GLITCH POETICS

Nathan Allen Jones

The **MEDIA : ART : WRITE : NOW** series mobilises the medium of writing as a mode of critical enquiry and aesthetic expression. Its books capture the most original developments in technology-based arts and other forms of creative media: AI and computational arts, gaming, digital and post-digital productions, soft and wet media, interactive and participative arts, open platforms, photography, photomedia and, last but not least, amateur media practice. They convey the urgency of the project via their style, length and mode of engagement. In both length and tone, they sit somewhere between an extended essay and a monograph.

Series Editor: Joanna Zylinska

GLITCH POETICS

Nathan Allen Jones

()
OPEN HUMANITIES PRESS

London 2022

First edition published by Open Humanities Press 2022

Print ISBN 978-1-78542-114-3
PDF ISBN 978-1-78542-113-6

OPEN HUMANITIES PRESS

Open Humanities Press is an international, scholar-led open access publishing collective whose mission is to make leading works of contemporary critical thought freely available worldwide.
More at http://openhumanitiespress.org/

Contents

Acknowledgements

A great deal of the work here was conceived through the PhD programme at Royal Holloway University of London, using a grant awarded by the university. Thanks to all the staff who made this possible, especially my supervisors Will Montgomery and Olga Goriunova for the time and energy they put into this project, and the transformative comments they made on early drafts. Thanks also to my examiners Peter Middleton, and of course Joanna Zylinska who subsequently invited me to prepare this manuscript for publication, and who, along with the rest of the OHP team, has provided excellent stewardship of the book.

Opportunities to present early versions of this work at the Bluecoat, Liverpool; Transmediale, Berlin; Electronic Literature Organisation events in Bremen and Cork; Onassis Centre in Athens, and Lancaster University, have been invaluable. The same goes for teams behind events in the extraordinary UK poetry, sound and media art scenes, where I was able to test and experience first-hand many of the creative ideas I write about here: Maintenant/Camerade, Penned in the Margins, Deep Hedonia, Café Ono, Gramophone

Raygun, my own collaborators on Mercy and Torque activity and Static Gallery in Liverpool, where a lot the first drafts were written. Thanks to everyone involved in those events and organisations, particularly those who extended invitations and friendship, and the people who took the time to share their own thoughts on my nascent ideas. Particular thanks go to my close collaborators, friends and mentors, Mark Greenwood and Sam Skinner.

Chapter 1 includes material that was originally published in *Bloomsbury Handbook of Electronic Literature*, ed. Joseph Tabbi (2017). Parts of the chapter regarding speed readers were also developed at Transmediale/Aarhus University workshop in Brussels in 2016 convened by Geoff Cox and Christian Ulrich Anderson, and published as the collaborative essay 'Absorbing Texts', co-written with Sam Skinner, first in *A Peer Review Journal About Machine Research* (2017) and then in *Back Office Journal* (2018).

In Chapter 2, material on Ben Lerner was also developed at a Transmediale/Aarhus University workshop, this one in 2016 in Liverpool. This work was published in *A Peer Review Journal About Excessive Research* (2016). Some of the material on Keston Sutherland was first published as 'Notes Towards a Glitch Poetics', edited by Frances McDonald and Whitney Trettien.

In Chapter 3, components on Ryan Trecartin and Jennet Thomas were first published in an article titled 'Glitch Poetics' in *Art Monthly* back in 2015, edited by Patricia Bickers.

Finally, thanks to my wife Nina.

Prologue

Two grainy photos appear in the gallery of my mobile phone: a meat pie; two children asleep on a large bed (fig. 1a&b). Both pictures have a sinister quality. The pie looks disgusting; the children look as though they have been thrown there. Something is wrong, but it is impossible to separate the wrongness of what is in each image from why I see them at all.

The pictures themselves are glitch messages, arriving unbidden in my phone's photo gallery; they feel wrong. They stop me and give me the sensation that *I* am being watched sleeping, *my* meals observed from above, or that I am somehow leading another life to which these digital sigils give me access, if only I can decode them. This 'glitch' is technology working correctly. In this case, it's the WhatsApp mobile messaging application automatically downloading images sent by friends of friends in group messages: an efficiency function I did not know existed. It freaks me out.

The phone rings. It is a female voice speaking quickly and insistently about car insurance. After the first few words, I have recognised that it is likely not a human on the other end of the phone. But, perversely,

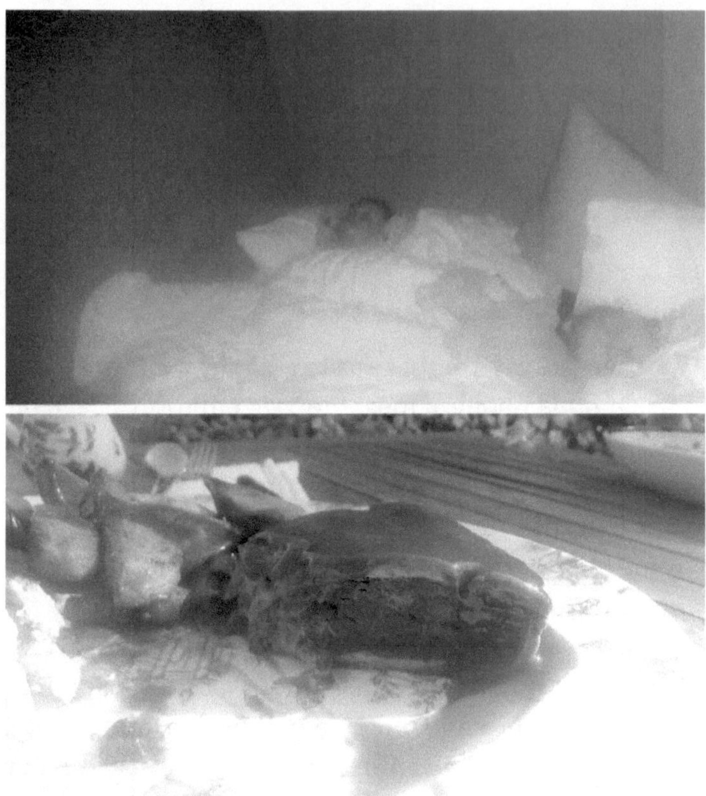

Figs. 1a and 1b. Images from author's phone.

not wanting to be rude, I hesitate. The microphones on the other end of the line register this gap and prompt the machine to adopt a different tone: *hello?... hello?* The voice granulates, slurs with a machinic affectation of concern. There is something in the grain of the words that tugs at my sympathy, even as it convinces me it is a machine speaking. What I'm hearing is an automated message, but rather than a pre-recorded voice, the script is composed uniquely for me; a synthesis made of thousands of recordings of human voices cut up into micro-second-long grains that flock into speech-like shapes and are modulated according to algorithmic instructions based on a written script.[1] I hang up, still faintly uncomfortable that someone, somewhere, will feel offended.

I turn back to my computer. I have a browser open with twenty separate tabs, some for news sites, blogs, journal or gallery websites, and several for different social media accounts, online teaching environments; another portal containing my details for payment and contract management, and another with which we book appointments with our students – portals within portals, and portals to access those portals. Layered on top of these windows on my laptop screen, I have documents in a word processor, my email server, some text files and a spreadsheet open. Words processing and being processed. Alerts, auto-update messages, windows that have frozen or crashed. I have forgotten what I am doing, but my body tells me I am working via the tension running across my shoulders and back. The diary in my email pings to notify me that a virtual meeting that I have to attend has started. I click, and the video streams of my colleagues in their rooms appear on the screen, streaming into mine. I can hear them speaking. Faces freeze and release blossoms of pixelated movement. They become scuzzy with colour-bleed and bright and clear again as the network and computer hone and auto-correct their buffering rate, graphics handling. The sound is not working. As they talk, I turn on the auto-captioning. 'Welcome everyone. Sweet boy. Has anyone got any comments on the minutes of the last. Meeting?' More silence.

I close the meeting, and the browser appears. The Facebook tab shows a number, indicating that I have numerous notifications. Relief, but also anxiety. The rhythm of the hour shifts a little; I am made torpid, scrolling down through various anomalies, none with sufficient force to disrupt my sense of normality: now spinach can send email; the arctic ice shelf has not begun freezing, weeks late; people from an image-posting board have bankrupted the stock exchange; a refugee camp in Greece is burned to the ground; water is discovered on the moon, a silver monolith appears in a Utah desert. Glitches proliferate. The world appears unsustainable, infested by temporary fashions, fragile, stuck in weird semantic loops, vulnerable to spikes in electrics and code, temporary and contingent.

> *Sainz thought Bahrain GP qualifying 'was over' after Q1 glitch, A GLITCH on a surf skiers phone led Southend Coastguard to launch a rescue mission, Hubble Space Telescope is back online after software glitch, Zoom Screen-Sharing Glitch 'Briefly' Leaks Sensitive Data, 3 Russian bomber pilots killed by ejection system glitch, TikTok users reported a For You Page glitch that sent them careening into 'straight TikTok', France's limited lockdown beset by glitches as cases rise, Data glitch 'may have led to more than 1,500 Covid deaths in England', Technical glitch halts trading on Japan's exchanges,*

> *Crypto exchanges glitch on bitcoin bounce after Tesla's $1.5bn investment, Facebook glitch wipes out hundreds of US election advert.*[2]

Finally, I check the source of the notifications by clicking on the red button. I have commented on a popular political blog. I have been accused of being a Tory troll, a racist, a paedophile within a few comments as I read. Like with the phone call, some of these messages may not be written by people but rather are posted by 'bots' – fake accounts powered by rudimentary artificial intelligence – or 'trolls', malicious actors who post content intended to rile and foment negative feeling. (The comments I receive on this posting are nothing compared to the abuse others receive on social media. Women, especially in media and politics, and particularly those who are racialised, are often singled out.) For the most part, even the slightest hint that a message is from a bot or troll will cause me to ignore the message and block or delete the user. But these hints, and so the attention I give to detecting them, often operate below the level of awareness and leave a trace on my sense of wellbeing. Just as the eye scans the face of an interlocutor in person, the mind trained to trace, suspect, process and act over thousands of years of evolution now strains for information from a few lines of text, hyper-aware of any deviant behaviour but also seeking out sincerity and well-meaning allies.

In the same fashion, when later I use the Google search engine, my eye takes in the headlines, titles and teaser content revealed by a search, seeking a trustworthy or at least time-worthy source. I look without seeking, as though sincerity sits on the surface text of these headlines, likewise relevance, truth: all detectable from experience in the small but complex array of variables offered on the search results screen. We have trained ourselves to not waste too much time on this chronic process of recall and discovery, but now this lack of time has itself been monetised and second-guessed. The powerful algorithm Google uses to search the internet and produce relevant links is partly informed by a constantly updated database of words with a financial value attached to them, so advertisers have anticipated my search, or something like it, and pre-emptively bought a space in my peripheral vision.[3] I instinctively try to tune them out, but of course, the same variables I use to search for valuable information can also be triggered to generate other responses – desire, curiosity, perhaps even disgust – by human and machine authors trained in 'search engine optimisation' techniques designed to tug at my will.

The calculated intimacy or emotional aggression of trolls, spambots and other malicious actors online, the grotesquely enticing word-salad of SEO-optimised headlines, the way that corporate decisions filter through into our textual environment and social sphere, the startling data on climate and social change, the prevalence and material cost of computer glitches, are unique to the moment I have written this book in. My mind and body teeter continually on the verge of moonlighting from their predestined purpose as attention, thought and emotion are monetised. All three have somehow responded by becoming in short supply, drawn on by actual jobs and by sustaining multi-billion-pound social media sites that rely on our life-material as 'content'. Networked computers in their current form, including as smartphones, are compulsively errant and colonising in this fashion, driving a distinctively, strongly deviating series of attention and care pathways into our predisposition by offering up small rewards, nudges and deflations back and forth between value and life, providing deflections in the form of glitches that take us outside of our intended route through our day.

In this book, glitches are slips, disruptions, errors and ambiguous hybrid states with a complex relationship to intentions and knowledge. We do not know where their meaning lies, so our feelings are drawn into the interpretative function. Glitches work to subvert and short-circuit intentions into their opposites: hindrance, aimlessness, lostness, but they also push into new forms of use, purpose and knowledge by revealing the nature of knowledge and feeling in relationship to technics. New technologies disrupt to form new patterns of thought and feeling that profit can be derived from, but disruptions in patterns of thought and feeling are also a method for liberation and critical use. Artistic disruptions hold us within the space of new technology, feeling and knowing differently. They invite us to identify the limits of intended profit patterns and even reveal hidden potentials in them: the useless and beautiful emerge from glitches, as do the scary and unimaginable.

The artistic glitch draws on the energy of disruption as a surprise event, but it is often the result of careful and attentive explorations of a given technology, even crafting. In *Glitch Poetics*, I look at how the experience of disruptive language technologies (as code software and digital storage, but also as social media feeds, emails and search engines) are tuned into surprise literary encounters by contemporary language artists, poets and novelists who craft their work to feel errant.

The majority of the detailed analysis in this book focuses on creative works made by media and literary practitioners in the early- and mid-2010s, a time when the term post-digital – and also post-internet – was entering the cultural vernacular. Kim Cascone coined 'the post-digital' in 2000 to refer to the aesthetics of error in glitch music. By the 2010s, it had been adopted in art and design and, vitally, its use had broadened to include not just an artistic response but a kind of condition: we were seemingly living in the aftermath of something, even as it came to predominate in almost every interaction. In a 2014 article, Florian Cramer suggested that the term post-digital 'sucks but is useful' because it refers to practices that historicise the digital illusion – of efficacy, speed, immateriality – and show how this illusion manifests as perversely inefficient, slow and unwieldy technologies. In retrospect, we can see that the use of 'glitch' and 'post-digital' as terms for a kind of creativity of the 2010s, particularly practices emphasising the exhaustion and inescapability of computational and networked technologies, was indicative of a socio-cultural boundary moment. Throughout the 2010s, the core illusions of the digital came unstuck. Wikileaks and Edward Snowden revelations about the massive data-capture strategies by US and UK governments showed that the internet was a space in which our every communicative interaction was being monitored, along with our location and identity. In 2016 the use of the same data-scraping and 'leak' technologies was used by Russian and hard-right campaign groups – themselves associated with the Wikileaks platform – to hack the national elections in the US and the Brexit referendum in the UK. In far-right campaign groups, racist and violent messages proliferated with sufficient ambiguity to evade the laws set up to censor such activity; hidden in plain sight as a cartoon of a green frog, a series of brackets surrounding a name, an 'ok' emoticon, the genie of white supremacy was out of the bottle, embodied in the new president of the USA. Practically also, the internet and the digital technologies that are attached to it have come to be acknowledged with a gritted-teeth realism, rather than the sense of possibility that they originally had. The mobile phone is a regular fixture at dinner tables and bedside tables across the globe, and a cause of arguments, neck, arm, back and eye pain. Many writing, publishing and reading institutions have been disrupted, replaced by automated, 'self-driven' and online computational counterparts; a marketplace that started out as an online bookseller has become the largest company on the planet, dominating electronic and physical book sales and branching out in to military technology, internet infrastructure, and ... everything. The digital is 'all over', in the sense that it has become embedded in every aspect of our lives. The privacy and security issues briefly awakened in the mid-2010s are now part of the general atmosphere of suspicion, disillusion, self-awareness and self-management that we work and think in today. The 2010s were 'a period in which our fascination with [digital] systems and gadgets [became] historical' (Cramer 2014). As I finish a day of Zoom meetings in my bedroom and immediately reach for my phone, reading on there that a computer glitch may have led to the deaths of over a thousand people from a new deadly virus, I understand that I have indeed come to live in the aftermath of that illusion.

Here I analyse works from the fall of the digital age as rendered in 'real-time' in the literature. I use the term 'glitch' in combination with poetics to describe a number of literary works of this era because the background processes of authorship were irrevocably embedded during this time into the same digital and networked technology processes as new media art. I suggest that literary and media innovations and experiments, glitch language and media together produce modes of language practice that can re-fascinate us in the digital world and bring it into question once again.

INTRODUCTION

Media Realism in Post-Digital Writing

'Glitch poetics' is a mode of reading and writing language errors in contemporary literature in ways that reflect something new about our encounters with digital technology. It is an emergent literary style, a media realism in which literary language is entangled in today's hyper-mediated conditions, making them speak about the way things are and will be as we integrate digital technologies ever deeper into our lives. In media art, the glitch is recognised as an aesthetic arising from between-states, alternative connectivities and misuse. Glitches illustrate connections between circuit interference and power-level surges, moments that codes err and loop, pixel-level image distortions and audio granulations, voices and faces that slur and music or patterns that crumble. In time these ambiguous, ruined, blooming between-states produce new understandings, new forms of use that slide between our pre-conditioning on what computers can and should do, and what we fear or desire about them. Glitch poetics carries the movement and temporary quality of the glitch, which Rosa

Menkman (2011) calls the 'glitch moment(um)', into contemporary literature, an area of practice that shares multiple porous boundaries with the digital realm in which glitches are born. As with the aesthetic errors of media art, the deliberate errors in glitching literature translate the oddly errant media conditions of our time into a readable form: exposing us and deepening our understanding of the ways computational and networked technologies err and falter.

Error and Unknowing

Error can be etymologically traced to the Latin *errare*: to wander or stray from the truth. But, as I have suggested in the prologue to this book, the sense that something is *becoming wrong* has perversely become one of the most emphatic truths of our time. Things *feel wrong* in a world where computers speak, write, package and programme information; when the world is stratified by software and algorithms that update without our knowledge, pressuring our minds and bodies into shapes and patterns over durations we are not used to; when we are habituated into the use of devices and tools that we have little understanding of and that update more quickly and persistently than we can keep up with.

Historically error has also found moral echoes in its synonym: deviance. The deviant strays from the path circumscribed by written and unwritten laws, living in the shadowy between-spaces, unmapped areas of cities, ethics and networks. Deviants pay the price by giving up the protections and privileges of society. The digital error likewise circumvents the laws that govern media and information flows, and in doing so shifts between and outside of normative laws, protections and allowances. Planetary scale digital platforms such as Google and Facebook glitch 'the laws of the land', deviating from taxation and freedom of information conventions established in relation to a world governed according to national boundaries. They pay the price by being refused access to their markets or shut down altogether for a brief moment before the system of technics and laws corrects itself around them (Kim 2012). Likewise, if we misuse our devices, open them up in the wrong way or submit them to unsuitable environmental conditions, we exit the protection of warranties and user recognition. But there is always the possibility that this will produce wider system-altering effects.

For some, manipulating digital technologies away from what they 'should' do into what they 'could' do becomes a political-artistic methodology. Artists who misuse digital media in this way are collectively called glitch artists (Beflix 2001, Moradi 2009, Temkin and Manon 2010, Menkman 2010, Cloninger and Briz 2015). The error of glitch art un-knows how media devices, software and our own bodily 'wetware' function, finding ways to untangle our creative mores from the increasingly complex behavioural nudges and habit-forming limitations of commercial applications. Part of recent media history, *glitch poetics* is a term I use to describe how the glitch proliferates as a tactic in literary and para-literary practice, carried like a virus through the networked and computational technologies that diffuse themselves into authorship, readership and publishing.

Bringing the terms glitch and poetics together will help me illustrate an affinity between glitch art and the long-standing engagements with impropriety, deviation and between-states in literature. Artists working in experimental poetry and the critical off-shoots of poetry called 'poetics' often conceive of language as a system of logics that can be bent and broken to deviate from the conditions of the sayable delimited by existing norms. Still, the reason the glitch/poetics affinity works so well today is that computational processes increasingly shape today's language norms. Computational media are linguistic at several layers of their operation. From interlocking layers of high, human-readable, and lower, machine-readable, codes, to the syntactically arranged stacks of technical components and interfaces that connect us to the network, to the distinctive vernaculars that emerge from technical expertise and the niche interest groups that flourish online, to the ways we embody the ticks and tropes of digital cultures in our everyday lives, each of these layers, types and modes of new media language can be glitched and are *glitch-y*. It is one of the functions of poetics today that it provokes us to consider the transformed situation for speaking, writing and thinking through experiments in poetry.

As the above suggests, glitch operates in another way in the book, offering a way out of 'poetics' as a discipline concerned with poetry and literary language, and giving it purchase on the wider world of interfaces and media. Glitching poetics means infecting, impurifying, diverting its concerns, finding between-spaces where it speaks to other disciplines, fields and modes of articulation. It also means pushing the tools of poetics up against modes of language practice outside of the literary. In my work, the critical arguments hover between analysis of poetry and literature, media use, media forms and theory, and artistic deployments of language in video art and performance. In this way, the book seeks a purchase that, as I show, much contemporary poetry does have, but the criticism around it rarely offers. Likewise, as a book of media aesthetics, the work finds a potency by deviating into literary theory and literary analysis in ways that provide a new intellectual vector for a term that was predominantly thought in DIY art practice.

From Hitch to Glitch

Glitches are woven through media histories as modes of disruption and subsumption in ways that bind different moments of human-technology, human-language and technology-language interface. The first use of 'glitch' has commonly been attributed to John Glenn in his 1962 account of the Project Mercury space expedition, referring to 'a surge of current or a spurious electrical signal', as 'slang for hitch' (Glenn 1969, 43), from where it was assumed that it expanded to include a broader array of technical errors. But a 2013 posting by Ben Zimmer reveals that the term was initially used to describe a human mistake and was possibly drawn etymologically from the Yiddish *glitchen,* standing for a language slip. Zimmer quotes a 1952 text by the actor Tony Randall of his time on the radio: ' When an announcer made a mistake, such as putting on the wrong record or reading the wrong commercial, anything technical, or anything concerning the sales department, that was called a "glitch" and had to be entered on the Glitch Sheet' (Zimmer 2013).

From the join between the radio announcer's mouth and broadcasting apparatus prosthetics, the term migrated into television technologies and corporate culture, where it was used in trade adverts to refer to the horizontal banding on television screens or the 'jiggles' visible from video edits. Bleeding into computer culture, glitch is still often used to refer to the artefacts of interference, traces or patterns that surge, mistakes and misuse they give rise to, but rarely is it acknowledged that a human misspeaking, mistyping – or misinterpreting – can cause these. Through computers, the glitch has entered our everyday lives: now that we are all producers, announcers and corporations, the frustrations and curiosities of on-screen errors are all too familiar.

In the 1990s, creatives began to exploit signs of digital interference as forms of aesthetic production, firstly in music in the work of experimental practitioners such as Oval and Kim Cascone. They used purposefully broken CDs and overloaded sound-compression modules to add a media-specific texture to their 'glitch

Fig. 2. Beflix, ENDEMEROL, 2001. Courtesy of the artist.

aesthetic' sound. Following this, visual artists such as Beflix (Ant Scott) began to produce images by 'circuit bending' and otherwise interfering in hardware-software interfaces in digital image-making tools, creating a manifestly errant digital style of noisily patterned abstract art (fig. 2). Beflix was the first person to coin the term 'glitch art' to describe the images he made by running code errors through mixtures of analogue and digital interface and screen-capturing the results.

The textures and patterns of pixilation on a malfunctioning digital screen operate in contradiction to mainstream digital culture. The commercial products of the digital are commonly associated with high resolution, faultless, 'smooth and clean' imagery and sound, but glitches present another, perhaps deeper, perspective on this set of technologies. Olga Goriunova and Alexei Shulgin (2008) state that the artefacts of glitch are, in fact, the 'aesthetics of digital systems' themselves. Absent the human announcer, the glitch has come to denote how the digital speaks itself, the truth of our systems delivered in an authentic vernacular emerging from within networks and circuitry. 'A glitch is a mess that is a moment' (Goriunova and Shulgin 2008, 114) when one layer of media production reveals itself as corruption or impurity on another, this mess-state cascades through material, data and human interfaces before the system crashes or corrects, finishing the moment it began. The idea that the digital reveals something before it is corrected is also linked to the notion of deviance and mis-speaking: when caught in the act of 'leaking' information from the interior of any system, one is quickly shut up (or rather down).

Methods for making the digital itself speak have proliferated along with the massive diversity of modes by which the digital translates media. In Takashi Murata's film *Untitled (Pink Dot)* (2007), extracts from a digitised copy of the 1982 Sylvester Stallone film *Rambo* are digitally processed as data, removing information in their code to the degree that the playback artefacts become the dominant visual component of the viewing experience. Murata's central character is the silicon Rambo, emerging from the network of pirate copies and streaming services.[4]

In Murata's 'datamoshed' videos, the interpretation of these artefacts can suggest aesthetic or political trajectories. The aesthetic reading favoured by gallery texts emphasises the uncanny weirdness and foreground-background, movement-form hybrids in ways that hark back to the writing on abstract art. An

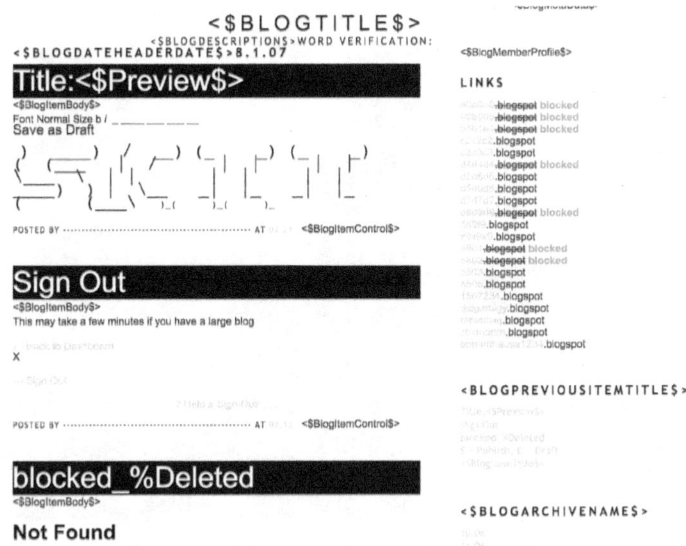

Fig. 3. Screenshot from Jodi's <$blogtitle$>, 2017. Used with permission.

example of this is Rhizome's *Artbase*, which describes Murata's work as 'creating undulating and living fields of video' (Rhizome 2014). Conversely, the critical media reading will emphasise the shift in audience literacy in these works' spectatorship. Interpreted by Brown and Kutty (2012),[5] *Untitled [Pink Dot]* illustrates a relationship between keyframes and pixel movements, elements that we typically encounter as a homogenous surface effect.

Prominent examples of the art that has emerged from a lineage of glitch and that emphasises media literacy include Jodi's *<$blogtitle$>* (2006) (fig. 3), in which the artist duo hack their own Blogger website so that it shows its HTML code, or Nick Briz's *Glitch Codec Tutorial* (2010) (fig. 4), where he tweaks (and tells the user how

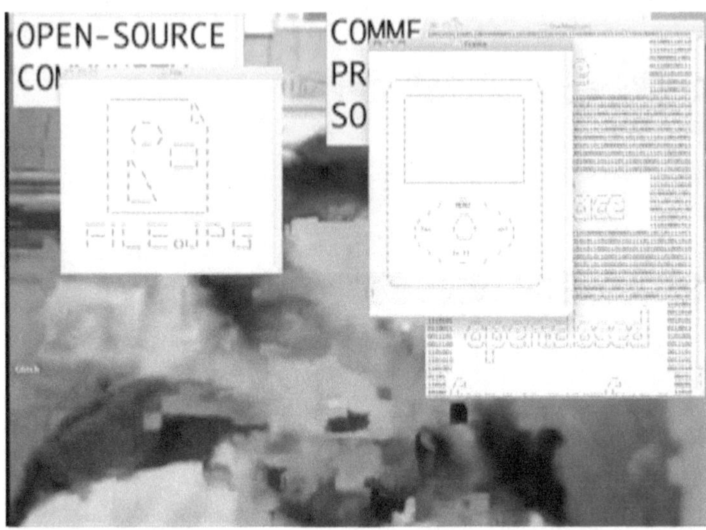

Fig. 4. 'As technologies "upgrade" and error checking protocols hoard in, this particular glitch may cease to exist'. Screenshot from Nick Briz's Glitch Codec Tutorial, 2010.
Used with permission.

to tweak) an Apple Mac media player so that videos become infested with patterns of the codec algorithms that play them.

In the 'second wave' of glitch art, artists such as Nick Briz and Rosa Menkman, Jon Satrom, Daniel Temkin, Jon Cates in Chicago, and Daniel Rourke and Antonio Roberts in the UK came together around 'dirty new media' GL.IT/CH festivals, testing a range of modes and methods for glitching that combine the aesthetic originality of gallery circuits with the critical sensibility of technical cultures and media theory. It was in workshops at these festivals that Curt Cloninger proposed that language could be glitched via conceptual, procedural and writing constraints. Putting glitches in tension with notions of the utterance and experimental performance practice resulted in some useful written work on this topic.

In *Gltchlnguistics: The Machine in the Ghost / Static Trapped in Mouths*, Cloninger observes that glitches break down the dichotomy between hardware and software, illustrating that they are 'rigorously, fine-grainedly, contingently enmeshed' (Cloninger 2010). He says language can also be broken down by glitches, forming an ambiguous space between the dichotomy of the language system and its instantiation in 'real-time' utterances. Cloninger observes that when we glitch language through media, our desire to decode a meaning is activated but overburdened, and that it is combined with the excess affective qualities of the utterance. He gives the example of Menkman's *Dear Mr Compression* (fig. 5), in which Menkman deploys glitch-codec techniques to make her writing partly illegible. This work is an excellent example for a theory of glitch based in the utterance. Because it is time-based, there is no particular need to distinguish between the various modes of utterance in it (Menkman's writing, the text appearing on the video screen, the reader's encounter with this text and its subvocalisation), and the way they augment the linguistic content.

We experience the overflow of the digital materiality in this work as an 'affective force' that becomes entangled with the symbolic meaning of the language. The disruption of the video codec interplays with the

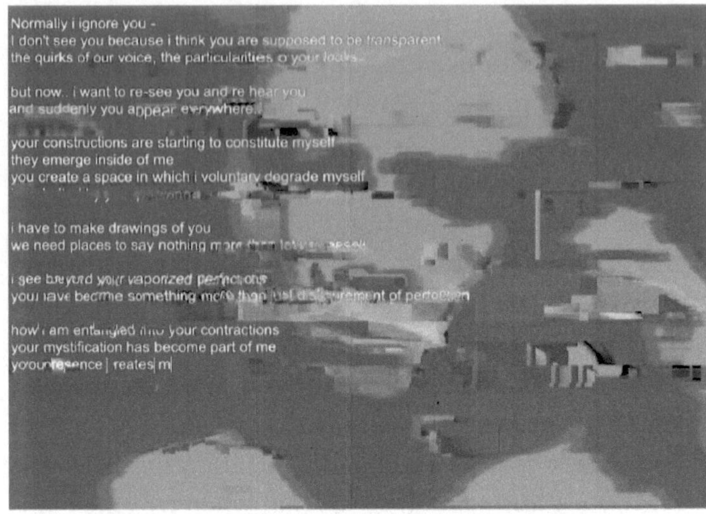

Fig. 5. Screenshot from Rosa Menkman's Dear Mr Compression, 2010. Used with permission.

content of the language, giving an acute 'feeling' to the narrator's desire to communicate with her interlocutor (is it really the codec she is addressing, or us?), while only ever being partially understood. Cloninger's writing suggests that once the digital system becomes involved in the process of utterance, then there is a progressively deepening entanglement of language and media expressing itself in more subtle and fine-grained types of distortions. I want to push this observation further by exploring how glitches that do not foreground any meaningful digital role in writing or reading nonetheless reveal digital qualities as excesses of affect, texture and wrong-feeling.

Glitch Momentum, Digital Vernacular

Menkman has since emerged as a prominent artist-theorist in glitch art's second wave, at least in Europe. She has written two books that identified the epistemology (*Glitch Studies* 2010) and phenomenology of the glitch (*The Glitch Moment(um)* 2011). Her subsequent artistic works, such as *Institution of Resolution Disputes* (2019), extend the form of error-enquiry into a broader political-aesthetic project. In *The Glitch Moment(um),* Menkman combines the weird technical (nonhuman) and aesthetic (human) moment of the glitch by suggesting that glitches are, in fact, 'critical sensory' encounters: the glitch moves between modes of affective and cognitive interaction. The glitch event's tangible form propels us into new kinds of understanding and interaction with usually hidden aspects of devices and software, she suggests, in much the same way that energy surges propel the computer into new manners of articulating electronic signals on a screen. The glitch is an interface between human and machine in a state of emergency or weakness for both, and it is a tipping point between operation and failure when destruction leads to discovery: 'Within the constructed ruins of glitch, new possibilities and new meanings arise. There is something more than just destruction: new understandings lie just beyond the tipping point. The glitch generates new understandings of techno-culture through the gestations of Glitchspeak, glitch's constantly growing vocabulary of new expressions' (Menkman 2011, 43).

Menkman says of the computer glitch that it makes us 'aware of the preprogrammed patterns' of our relationship to media in the moment of its error, when we cannot use something as expected. As a result, she suggests that in the wake of a glitch, 'a distributed awareness of a new interaction gestalt can take form' (Menkman 2011). This means that a new way of producing and imagining the world emerges from breaking and distorting what an interface or device can do or show. Likewise, in this book I will ask of particular poems and other unwieldy language-moments what kind of 'interaction 'gestalt' takes form in their wake. In other words, I will examine how the world of the sayable is re-distributed across language and technology by faulty literary propositions.

As the extracts above show, Menkman frequently casts the media-weirdness of glitches in linguistic terms. For Menkman, language is a figure for the structuring of experience that allows it to be interfaced with machines: glitches 'teach the speaker something about the inherent norms, presumptions and expectations of a [new media] language' (2010, 10). This is partly because it is code – the computer's 'native language' – that lies beneath the surface of our every interaction with digital media, but also because media itself can be thought of as a new kind of language in the manner it is strung together as syntaxes of operational units. Lev Manovich's *The Language of New Media,* which posits media arrays as constituting a language, 'an umbrella term to refer to a number of various conventions used by designers of new media objects to organise data and structure the user's experience' (Manovich 2011, 7), and which emphasises the diverse range of vectors for compatibility and connection new media give rise to, is also evoked in Menkman's work. In another work, *A Vernacular of File Formats* (Menkman 2010b), Menkman casts various compression formats for digital video and images as 'vernaculars', or accents, in which a media image is spoken through the machine.[6] With 'vernacular', Menkman suggests another similarity between spoken language and media: namely, that media is embedded in material conditions, traditions, genealogies of use and process, and that it is subject to social and environmental distortions in a way analogous to local and specialist human languages.[7] The limit of what is sayable has repercussions for a political identity that is a form of network compatibility. Driven through a practical experience of digital-analogue technology, the philosophical notion that language delimits the realm of experience and produces spontaneous networks of meaning is conceived through the particular contents and meanings of media: media errors, like language slippages, open up what is possible.

Experimental Realist

Writers are engaged in producing a new 'interaction gestalt' (Menkman 2011) for language that can articulate the overlap between humans, literature, code and the machines that run it. Some contemporary writers embody new media in their writing style by invoking the 'fragmenting' effect of pixelated images or granulating audio in their depiction of a mind in crisis, or using the imagery of buffering, stalling videos to suggest a memory half-recalled, half lost to the past. In *Red Pill* by Hari Kunzru (2020), the internet-induced psychosis of the central character manifests itself in a digital fragmentation: 'At the edges of my vision, the world seemed approximate, pixelated'. D. B. C. Pierre splits his novel *Meanwhile in Dopamine City* (2020) into two columns to reflect the incessantly distracting quality of the internet and the panicked quality of online reward-seeking that the title alludes to.

This invocation of technologically-induced distortions and pressures on the reading apparatus is a sign that the modernist impulse to make writing which breaks with tradition has been caught up by a media reality that seeks breakage as part of its operation. The Futurist poet Filippo Tommaso Marinetti's 1912 poetry book *Zang Tumb Tuum* attempted to 'free language' from the grid of the page, 'exploding the harmony of the page' (Danchev 2011) through onomatopoeia and graphical text arrangements, to translate the poet's experience of war machines. Marinetti glorified the disruptive potential of war machines in his visual poetry. The words splayed across the pages of *Zang Tumb Tuum* were 'futurist' in that they sought to use the disruption of war to project poetry away from tradition, and accelerate an imminent reality in which machinic technologies had social force. Marinetti's contemporaries depicted him writing and performing in a kind of 'deranged' intensity in which he sought to mimic the rapidity and noise of machine-gun fire, embodying the acceleration of the human absorption of machinic qualities that are lauded today as advances in labour and entertainment fields. As he put it in another manifesto text:

> a roaring motor car which seems to run on machine-gun fire, is more beautiful than [classical Greek sculpture] the Victory of Samothrace ... We are on the extreme promontory of the centuries! What is the use of looking behind at the moment when we must open the mysterious shutters of the impossible? Time and space died yesterday. We are already living in the absolute, since we have already created eternal, omnipresent speed. (Marinetti in Danchev 2011, 80)

Contemporaneously the poet Aldo Palazzeschi used a more playful 'plot-less flow of alliterations, rhymes, assonances, and consonances' (perhaps mimicking the schizophrenic's word-mania 'clanging', but also new kinds of data-patterning found in the city-surface by machine learning, for example) to replicate and articulate the noisy semiotic environment of the modern city (Tenenbaum 1986).[8]

As Friedrich Kittler (1999) observes, the unsettling quality of modernist literature in the first half of the twentieth century was entwined with recording technologies, and with human breakdown. Gertrude Stein had a typist to whom she dictated many works that anticipated the 'loop' that would characterise new musical composition, in particular, the 'minimalist music' in the coming decades (Deville 2013). Her *Geography and Plays* combines qualities of the seriality of language with the technics of nascent film technology in a way that deviates from literary norms:

> She was one and that was a thing that if it had been a sad thing would have been a sorrowful thing. She was one and that was a thing that if it had been an unpleasant thing would have been a disagreeable thing. She was one and if that thing had been a successful thing it would have been an interesting thing. She was one and if that thing had been a vigorous thing it would have been a continuous thing... (Stein 1922)

As Michael J. Hoffman (1965) observes, the phrases in this early work 'echo each other, as in the frames of a movie, each sentence substantially repeats its predecessor with an alteration in a key word or phrase to give a sense of both repetition and movement'. Stein renders the material and cognitive world of then-new media as an aesthetics of error, challenging us to recalibrate our interaction gestalt with words as readers. Similarly, throughout the twentieth century, practices such as William Burroughs and Brion Gysin's cut-up and tape-splicing works, Hart Crane's 'deranged' alcohol-and-gramophone fuelled, ornately complex poems (Reed 2004, 104), the 'dirty concrete' typewriter and sound experiments of Steve McCaffery's Carnival poems (fig. 6), the New York poets' dreamlike evocations of cities infused with growing intensities of media celebrity and aesthetics, and Kathy Acker's punk novels

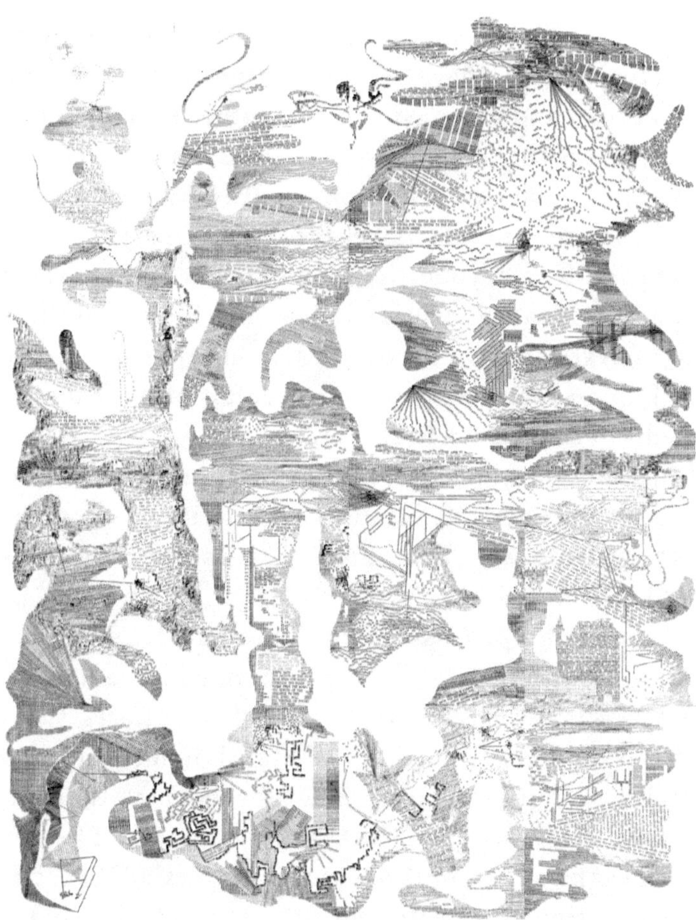

Fig. 6. A panel from Steve McCaffery's Carnival 1, 1967-1970. A 'dirty concrete' poem made with a typewriter. 'The page ... ceases to function as an arbitrary receptacle ... becoming instead the frame, landscape, atmosphere within which the poem's own unity is enacted and reacted upon. Page and type function as the two ingredients in a verbal sculpture' (McCaffery and Nicol 1992). Used with permission.

detourning high and low cultures of the postmodern in visceral style, have led the lineage of experimental modernist and postmodernist literature into the information age through corporeal excess. Each developed the early modernists' attempts to translate technological change into new language forms, breaking with the past. It is beyond the scope of this book to trace how technical innovations map onto historical literary movements. For the most part, the emphasis here is on human-read error and its interplay with the digital media of the twenty-first century.

In the techniques of looping, malfunction and language derangement established and iterated by the experimental artists of modernist traditions, today's writers find new ways of articulating how the digital codes and processes running at the threshold of our attention feel. Deviating from normative literary constructs in search of techno-aesthetic affects, these writers deploy intensities of Steinian seriality and Palazzeschian assonance, intensities that have the compulsive quality of runnable code (as I observe of Keston Sutherland's *Odes to TL61P* [2013]) or McCafferyesque malfunction, cut-paste and remix tactics to evoke a corrupt data-file (as I show of Ben Lerner's *Mean Free Path* [2010]).

Techniques involving breaking syntactic arrangements of texts have the effect they do now because we have internalised digital glitches as the likely source of malfunction in our world – for example, in our day-to-day experience of faulty, erratic 'advances' in word processing and email software. The glitch poetics works of the 2010s, particularly during the explosion of smartphone, email and social media use during this decade, mark the moment in which media breakdown became a personal issue. For this reason, the temporalities, textures and forms of the digital – in particular, the layers of automated and networked language tools, themselves continually breaking down, updating and exceeding our expectations – have jumped into the space opened up by modern and postmodern poetic invention.

As a result of the rapidity of technical change and its complex relation to literary innovation, there has emerged a generation of poets, novelists and para-literary 'experimental' writers who, unexpectedly perhaps, find themselves working at the intersection of realism, in that they render the social condition through the lens of individual experiences (Chase 1997). The methodologies of experimental writing, always partly disruptive in character, have now been caught up by the demands of realism in an environment seething with disrupting technologies. We read something real, something very much true, when narrative structures and sentences dissolve or fragment in ways that were received as mere language games only a few years ago. This offers experimental writing and the field of poetics a new entry point to the world. It is in the manifest strangeness of our lives, entwined ever more tightly with 'leaky' and 'creepy' (Chun 2016) technologies, that the poetics of media disruption converge with glitch art. One of the crucial aspects of this book is its attempt to show how the ever-more-subtle ways technology manifests in our lives result in innovative stylistic responses by writers.[9]

Leaky Creepy Media

The feeling that *something is wrong* has been normalised by our experiences of technology. The seemingly new is illuminated by the glitch, in that we certainly notice something anew when it breaks down, but also newness itself produces glitch-like encounters. These are commonplace in a world where disruptive kinds of newness are coupled with notions of commercial growth and 'market share'.

It is widely observed that disruption is one of the hi-tech industry's operating principles. In 2011 the investor Marc Andreessen wrote an influential article in the *Wall Street Journal*, stating, 'Over the next 10 years, I expect many more industries to be disrupted by software, with new world-beating Silicon Valley companies doing the disruption in more cases than not'. For Andreessen, the primary location of this disruption was to be the labour market, but more recently it has been the physical behaviours and mental ticks of users, and collective social norms, that have been disrupted in the name of hi-tech profit. The technologies that underpin the digital disrupt and are disrupted continually. This condition creates a tension between the level of absorption and openness, depth and surface we experience in them, which glitch practice has turned into an aesthetic principle. I am interested in how these aesthetics manifest in literature.

In *Updating to Remain the Same*, Wendy Chun (2016) describes new media as 'wonderfully creepy', capturing the promiscuousness with which new media devices – particularly smartphones – diffuse themselves into our lives and the weird sensations that result. Google CEO Erik Schmit has reputedly suggested that 'Google policy is to get right up to the creepy line and not cross it' (Saint 2010), but, of course, this belies Google's role in producing and moving that line. While only intermittently crossed, the creepy line is pushed into ever more proximate and complex relation to our physical and psychological interiors by glitches. Chun contends that, along with the line between creepy and not-creepy, numerous categories of propriety are disrupted by networked computational media. As well as 'creepy', the world of new media is 'leaky': its borders and boundaries are porous by design.

One of the critical creeping lines for Chun is the line that separates public from private. '[A] networked personal computer is an oxymoron. ... New media erode the distinction between the revolutionary and the conventional, public and private, work and leisure, fascinating and boring, hype and reality, amateur and professional, democracy and trolling (Chun 2016, 12). In Chun's view, it is no more possible to envisage a leak-free internet than a newness-free media industry. As a community of users, we are comfortable with the kinds of disruption generated by the data-capture-and-display capacities of our phones. We take it as a given that leaked privacy and disrupted attention are part of the price we pay for the conveniences they purport to offer.

For David Berry (2011), the paradoxical experience of attention and information drifting and leaking is a symptom of computers' construction. Computer networks, and their networking to users, are compacts of heterogeneous and faulty, often incompatible, systems of software, hardware and wetware bodies, which have been combined in ways that are *only just* commercially viable: cheap, quick fixes for issues arising as media deepen their integrations into our lives. The computer codes inside our devices do not work without flaws as they balance our interactions with them against the affordances of the hardware they control. They also continually recover and adapt to the errors that are thrown up, 'oscillating' in and out of operationality. This oscillation has ripple effects on our involved attention, which flickers in and out of focus. Although nominally experienced as flow, our life in 'the code saturated environment' is striated by moments where we recognise the complexity of our devices, which 'causes us to suffer switching costs, [and] ... change our state of being in the world' (Berry 2011, 141). This switching cost is sometimes incurred at the level of attention, such as the ping of a text message that distracts us from reading a long-form essay, but it is also continually happening at lower levels of consciousness. We shift between states of recognising the odd nature of the technology we have before us and it drifting into the background of our involved use. As citizens of a computationally administered world, we are paradoxically familiar with the estrangement of the faltering machine, drawing it closer and becoming ever more deeply unsettled. Berry calls the resulting error-existence a 'glitch-ontology'.

Where Chun's theory of creepy media pushes against Berry's 'glitch ontology' is that she looks for a 'slower, more unnerving time of "new media"' (Chun 2016, xi) in which socially disruptive tech makes its way from subliminal distraction through our learned responses into collective forms of social structure. Rather than living in code-saturated environments, Chun suggests, we have become saturated by code. We habituate to disrupted norms and collectively embody them. So oscillations and corrections between error and function are always social to some degree. Media 'matter most: when they seem not to matter at all' (Chun 2016, 1) because they have passed into us and are temporalising, scaling or shaping our behaviours. Breakage is a useful marketing tool; it asks us to notice and register the arrival of a tool or function; but it is through the resulting habituation of bodies collaborating to produce a habituated society that media become most influential.

As I have suggested above, computational and networked technologies enclose their possibilities primarily through habituating us to particular uses rather than any specific limit on their capability. In fact, their capabilities are continually being upgraded via software runnables. The newest functions of technology are, for all intents and purposes, glitches as they are jammed into our relatively old circuits of behaviour and replaced at a rate we cannot keep up with.[10] In literature, readers' habits are always in tension with cultures of innovation, experiment and radicalism, forming patterns of deviation, embodiment and rupture that mirror, anticipate and trace those of the mediasphere. What glitch poetics offer to this situation is to produce new modes of apprehending and articulating the edges of media effects in what has become commonplace, and to question how media and other disruptive infrastructures – such as those of word processing software or the publishing industry – are shaping what we can say.

Chun's work is vital to a theory that seeks to account for cultural glitches because it focuses on media patterns as they move through individuals and their milieu. She narrates the 'slow time' of new media's absorption into what is no longer new and sets the scene for glitches that emerge as a kind of symptom or spasm in our collective language. She gives the example of the 'ghost vibrations' experienced by users habituated to the Blackberry phone, giving it the title 'crackberry' after the physical nature of the addiction to the device's interaction. The Blackberry alert has outlived the device itself but lives on 'undead' in our bodies, which await the dopamine hit of a message vibration. This slower and creepier time of media means that in our habituation to media environments, we are embodying the disrupted experience of others: 'Habit is publicity: it is the experience, the scar, of others that linger in the self. Habits are "remnants" of the past - past goals/selves, past experiences that live on in our reactions to the environment today, as we anticipate tomorrow. Through habit, we inhabit and are inhabited by alterity' (95). Habituation is an important concept for this book because it is the embodied form that the no-longer-new disruptive technology takes. Therefore it is the method by which technologies have more lasting social effects which glitch poetics practitioners highlight and push back against.

Each new technology introduced to us via the market is socially disruptive. Like a pebble dropped into the lake, these large ruptures are echoed in disruptions to our concentration in the form of notifications, breakdowns, updates and other intrusions on the surface of our attention. Media absorb us but, at a deeper level, we absorb them: firstly in the form of individual habits, then as collective social patterns. Glitched lyric poetry, performance writing and realist literature each in their own ways accelerate or amplify the glitch as an embodied or social condition, and use it to provoke futurist approaches: crashing the past as a set of literary tropes and offering a reset of the relationship between media and language.

There is an interplay between the usefulness of the 'new' device, the body entrained to use it and the attention activated by it. This interplay, in particular the way in which devices intersect with the transitory nature of linguistic and narrative norms, is what contemporary glitch poetics practitioners write through. The weird sensation of being 'lost' when a phone call drops out, the act of interpreting a video caller's voice as the software clips it and the face blurs and buffers, the job of correcting critical neologisms and author names in auto-transcriptions of lectures, each become part of the leaky techno-gestalt in which a glitch poetics reading takes place. Operating at one remove from technology as such, glitch poetics is a study of the 'creepier, slower' effects of habituation to devices through its impact on a collective language. Similarly to glitch art, these language methods capture, fake, copy, slow, amplify and synthesise errors native to the digital in ways that ask us to question where the edges of the digital lie. These aren't moments when an author makes software or hardware devices break, but they are moments in which an author captures and renders the qualities of hardware switching and software glitching into an authentically faulty grammar, narrative or metaphorical hierarchy, inviting us to turn our literary reading into a media analysis.

For Chun, the effects of promiscuous and colonising technologies as they creep into our lives are mostly undetectable, precisely because of the degree to which they have come to encompass what our lives *are*: its edges have moved well beyond our peripheral vision. With glitch poetics, looking at (and doing) contemporary language practices of error, we can get new forms of purchase on how computers inform our lives and infect our experiences, finding the edges of media, languages and entrained bodies. The latest technologies, according to this reading, are not solely bundles of code and hardware with which we interact, but rather species-altering effects, producing hybrid human and corporate-machine cultures through which we are expressed. Chun's writing is itself 'wonderfully creepy' because it can follow such aspects of technology shift through different fields. Likewise, with glitch poetics I look to trace particular technology elements back and forth from literary effects in what Rosi Braidotti describes as a 'posthumanities' or 'post-disciplinary' movement (Braidotti 2009). My work replaces the systems engineering beginnings of Chun with literary ones, starting with a world in which authors are, to various degrees, influenced by the technologies that leak into their compositional practices, before shifting into the production of new perspectives on media aesthetics.

Software Code Poetry

In *Words Made Flesh* (2005), Florian Cramer traces a genealogy of language practices which shows that 'algorithmic code and computations can't be separated from an often-utopian cultural imagination that reaches from magic spells to contemporary computer operating systems' (Cramer 2005, 8). Central to this genealogy are readings of ecstatic language practices, from the kabala to sixteenth-century religious ecstatic verse, to the Beat poems of Allen Ginsberg in the 1950s and 1960s, each proposing a direct effect of language on the human mind and body. For Cramer, executable software codes are as much part of a lineage of incantations and magic as they are of mathematics and logic.[11] It is in these literary and esoteric cultures that language's inherent algorithmic potency was explored before the invention of machines that could 'run it', and the existence of executable languages as spells and ecstatic poems showed that 'language can be computational in itself' (2005 , 124). This problematises the traditional distinction that digital specialists such as Daniel Temkin and Hugh S. Manon (2010) used to delineate the glitch territory, suggesting that the word 'loses potency' in the case of non-digital phenomena. Ironically, Temkin curates one of the best records of the diversity, ingenuity, perversity and glitchiness of coding cultures in ways that parallel these qualities in literature: the *Esoteric Codes* website includes multiple examples of artists and coders (and artist-coders) who have invented perverse, divergent and productively unworkable ways of talking to computers. Rather than being maintained by binaries with hardware or the analogue, the code exhibited on Temkin's website consists of algorithms and their deployment and use among '*imaginary or actual* machines' (Cramer 2005), cultures and operations. As with poetry, the error, deviance and contradictions of the glitch are key to this line.[12]

Cramer identifies a 'speculative imagination' in a continuum of runnable codes, castable spells and experimental language practice's own use of execution as a motif. Echoing Berry's notion of the glitch-ontology produced by code, he suggests that code concerns itself with transgressing and holding in balance a series of contradictions, such as '[r]eduction and totality, randomness and control, physics and metaphysics' often finding itself in the position of 'short-circuiting their opposites': 'Computer users know these obsessions well from their own fears of crashes and viruses, bloatware, malware and vaporware, from software 'evangelists' and religious wars over operating systems, and their everyday experience with the irrationality of rational systems' (6). This is to say, glitch writing in experimental literature embodies and echoes the fundamentally leaky, errant qualities of code and spell writing historically: this writing disrupts and is disrupted.

As the *Esoteric Codes* website shows, we can break down software into a heterogeneous range of practices and forms, experiments and dead-end play. Understanding this zone of practices necessitates hybrid forms of media-literary reading. With glitch poetics, I look to provide purchase for these analyses in contemporary literature. One writer cited by Cramer who bridges the gap between esoteric literature and code is Mez Breeze. Breeze blends human language with syntaxes and symbols from high-level codes in a language that she calls *mezangelle,* using it to write poetry that gestures towards the executable while retaining and emphasising its literary nature. The result is a glitchy, deviant hybrid that crystallises the computational and networked character of the very online human. As the blurb on the back of Breeze's *Human Readable Messages: Mezangelle 2007-11* describes Breeze's process: 'stitch 2gether standardised literary conventions ... with coded poetics steeped in digital-drenched communication' (Breeze 2011). In the extract below, a poem called 'N.ternet N.force [micro.paw(n)]officer', originally posted on a mail-list, coding mark-up symbols and other digital text detritus from the mail-list format corrupt the language and extrapolate the potential meanings within a line creating a back-and-forth reading, whose meanings unfold slowly in the user. The poem '[soft.launch.ing] (2003-06-29 09:16)' figuratively 'launches' rather than begins, and its lines contain permutations that require processing rather than reading:

> [n]tense + volu[me lowered thru smurf.juicing.
> it.up]te net use
>
> . re.D.fining s[ocial]earch online pick up [on]
> s[errage +crumbling c(l)ost cuttage]
>
> ...
>
> r[g]iven on a[na]rchism na na na na arch arch arch
> riven [fo]r[g]iven . me be
>
> (Breeze 2011, 41)

As with Murata's datamoshed videos, our first encounter with Breeze's poetry is as a surface replete with affect. The wit of Breeze's deployment of this mode in her writing is that it allows our intuitive response to this work to interface with the way we understand the character depicted in the text. The writing style is like vernacular speech from a life lived inside code, human speech layered with the particular symbolic textures of the mail-list form as though it is only halfway emerging from the network. Parentheses are used to combine and break words in the poem so that they contain productive indeterminacies – being both inside and outside the phrase. This neatly corresponds to the mutable quality of digital texts whose words are a click away from saying something different altogether. But perhaps the most striking aspect of Breeze's poems is their sensuous quality. In a close reading, Breeze forces a particular sensuousness through the difficulty of the language, meaning that the reading process of these machine-human lines appears to rasp and hiss. The word 'technical', for example, takes a short-circuit through 'terrible' and the vocable 'ara' in 'te {[rrible] [ara] }chnical', while 'arch engines' become 'textural' and 'architectural' in the neologism 'arch[i.texture]'. In this way, the difficulties and possibilities in reading the work become analogous to the difficulties and possibilities of absorbing the tendencies of machines into our bodies.

This poem was written in 2003, when networked and digital technologies were less popular, less seamlessly integrated into our lives and more overtly technical. More recently, art writer Linda Stupart has evoked the contiguity between magic and runnable code in the 'binding spells' directed at abusive male artists in her book *Virus* (2015). The spells draw on the witching tradition but also wittily juxtapose it with biological disease and techno-knowledge. Most of the spells interspersing the book's narrative involve rituals. 'A Spell to Bind Richard Serra', for example, instructs the user to burn a black candle and oils while holding a wrapped copy of the famous artist's work and speaking the spell '*Bound by twines, with this charm... / Bind Richard Serra, and his work, from doing harm...*' (58, italics in original)';[13] 'A

Spell for Binding a Super Trendy Sexist Hot Young Male Artist's Internet Access,' in turn, instructs the user to 'create an executable that will literally break their computer', instantiating a connectivity glitch:

> @Echo off
>
> Ip config. / release
>
> Save that as a .bat and send it to someone. Their IP address will be lost, and therefore they won't be able to fix it. (79)

Stupart's book makes an analogy between the redemptive, corrupting potentials of feminist rage and the magical-fantastical figure of the virus that crosses computer and biological forms using error. The book's action takes place at the boundary-point between computers and bodies, as glitches that are erotic and violent. Her virus has sex, 'glitches through another orgasm... twitches inside her diodes'. Like Breeze, Stupart recognises an inherently visceral quality in the notion of a machinic language that is runnable like code in the human body. However, in *Virus*, rather than *looking like* code, the figure of the virus *acts like* code: multiplying copies of itself, leaking across computer networks as a chat-room bot, and having agency at the interface of technology and humans – for example, in lecture theatres, where the human body is augmented by sound systems, and in digital recording set-ups, setting the scene for memorable moments of visceral violence in the book.

In the intervening years between Breeze and Stupart, the communicative relationships we have with digital devices has changed, and the community of digital users has exploded: both in the sense that it has expanded rapidly and also fragmented into innumerable new sub-communities, each with its own vernacular relationships to networked technology. The difficult boundary line between the computational and the physical remains, but in Stupart's work it has been sublimated into a dramatic conceit rather than serving as a lexical imperative.

Breeze's brand of hybridised, glitchy poetics now has a retro aesthetic. In their extreme timeliness to the period in which they were written, the poems hark back to a moment when timecodes, edit histories and HTML were still part of the experience of the 'everyday' media vernacular for the people who knew it best: whether in the case of a faulty browser, viral spam or in authoring their own Myspace pages, a user could be expected to see or use mark-up of this kind, and a fluency in code languages implied a sense of community. Breeze's work uses the glitch to produce a 'slang' of the early internet community, who read it as such.

As with glitch art's pixilations, the aesthetic possibilities of 'fake' coding conventions perhaps now appear kitsch. But more recent glitch poetics works like Stupart's work with ever-more rapid perversions, distortions and deviations of online vernaculars, keying into the current fears and assumptions about technologies that leak and creep into the body in ever more obscure ways. Now that computers understand and process our needs based on gesture and voice commands, and now that they proliferate into more aspects of our social interactions, new kinds of poetic response are required to identify and characterise them. Today's glitch poetics can characterise how it feels to live alongside – and inside – machines, and what it means to have them anticipate and augment our forms of expression.

In his 2015 poetry collection *Kim Kardashian's Marriage*, Sam Riviere includes the residue of media as a texture in his poems. Without the evident technical know-how of those authors, Riviere's work has a more obliquely digital nature than Breeze's or Stupart's, instead engaging in the unique quality of language cycles in pop culture. (The title is a reference to the seventy-two poems in the book, a poem for each of the days Kardashian was married before divorcing in 2011). The poem 'spooky weather' is typical, generating its spookiness from the ambiguity between the supposedly heartfelt, imagistic and 'genuine' combination of pathetic fallacy 'through your spine. Late October rain./ Drizzling down. Talent that touches your heart', and odd interventions, as though a computer was pushing out pre-written generic content 'This is a repost' ... 'I have to apologise if I'm not around the next few days' (Riviere 2015). Riviere's poems may not be visibly corrupted like Breeze's, or invoke code in the way that Stupart's do, but reading them we feel the 'wrongness' of today's mediatised language as an affect in a similar way. Something is intriguing and sensuous about the nature of this wrongness: it invites us to look again at what it means to write an email today, in the context of auto-reply and Google auto-complete messages, living through a browser which is alive with data-scraping technologies, as though poetic language has been depleted by this condition somehow. Breeze's, Stupart's and Riviere's work, though very different, could all be read as forms of Julia Kristeva's 'abject', being at once about the subject (human) and its object (computer): a form of boundary-writing that gives us a creepy sensation precisely because of its imprecise outlines. Contemporary practitioners whose work may appear to have little to do with the digital open their writing to computation through errors of this kind; their work feels wrong in a way that echoes our experience of techno-culture.

Literacy of Technology

Poetics is the critical-creative, self-reflexive companion to poetry's rich production of language worlds. It is inherently concerned with the conditions and means of its production and use: the systems, standards, politics and tendencies of language that inform how poetry feels. At its best, poetics is also a method that pushes poetry criticism into an engagement with the world, including a broader disciplinary scope than the academic study or commercial review of literature. The language poet Lyn Hejinian names a number of issues that poetics concerns itself with: 'poetic language puts into play the widest possible array of logics, and especially it takes advantage of the numerous logics operative in language, some of which take shape as grammar, some as sonic chains, some as metaphors, metonyms, ironies, etc. There are also logics of irrationality, impossibility, and a logic of infinite speed...' (Hejinian 2000, 3).

In the glitch poetics readings in this book, I will be looking for breaks with 'logics operative in language' and moments in which new logics are put into play to produce error effects that echo the glitch artist's work with digital systems. I will also try to use such readings to demonstrate that poetry gets a distinctive purchase on the world today via its engagement with media. The results of this engagement can be read as errors, but there are aesthetic and epistemological possibilities in them: alternative notions of what drives syntax and textual flow connect language breaks to our experiences of disruptive technology.

Alternative readabilities emerge in the wake of our encounters with breakdowns in established textual logics. For example, the 'logic of infinite speed' is hard to reconcile with readability, and 'sonic chains' can be experienced as an error in that they interfere with the comprehensibility of something that is being said (as in the case of schizophrenic clanging). These faulty readings operate as a synecdoche for alternative modes of interaction with the world at large. This possibility to rethink what is readable and question what reading means is a crucial aspect of poetic language. As Giorgio Agamben asks in *Art, Inoperativity, Politics*, 'What in fact is a poem if not a linguistic operation which renders language inoperative by de-activating its communicative and informative functions in order to open it to a new possible use?' (Agamben 2007, 140). For Agamben, it is precisely in its 'inoperativity' that poetry offers something new to the language we use. In the moment of literary malfunction, Agamben encounters a situation where 'language has been rendered inoperative and has become, in language and through language, purely speakable' (140). This phrase echoes the attempt of glitch artists to articulate the 'digital itself' and show how glitches reveal aspects of the systems they interrupt.

In later work, Agamben poignantly joins up his observations about the inherent 'inoperativity' in linguistically innovative poetry to write through the 'dark and maimed language' of Paul Celan's writing on Auschwitz, which articulates something that is beyond the expressive function of the sayable. In *Remnants of Auschwitz* (2012), Agamben deploys what he has learned from his long engagement with poetry as an investigation into linguistic limits to move beyond literary analysis, and into a philosophy of the limits of the human subject.

> This is the language of the 'dark shadows' ... in Celan's poetry, like a 'background noise' ; this is Hurbinek's non-language (mass-klo, matisklo) that has no place in the libraries of what has been said or in the archive of statements. (37) ... When the relation between ... the sayable and the unsayable, is broken in the subject, language dies and a new linguistic identity emerges. (160)

There are echoes here of Menkman's notion of a new interaction gestalt. Which is to say, Agamben views poets such as Celan as affective tacticians, forcing an examination of language that is simultaneously deeply personal and embedded in wider political questions through their willingness to break with its established literary norms.

Agamben's work in this area (as with Berry's notion of the glitch-ontology) is informed by the phenomenology of Martin Heidegger. Heidegger suggests a person is 'always already abandoned to a factual situation beyond which [they] can never venture' (Heidegger 2007 [1927], 126). He says people make their way through life using tools that become more unknown the more intimately entangled these tools become in their lives. This unknowability is only overcome at the moment that the tools we have 'ready-to-hand' break down, and our attention is deflected back to their capacities (127). The broken or faulty tool in Heidegger is the basis for the philosopher's later and less well-known writing on poetry. Echoing the tool theory in this writing, he suggests that the 'caesura-like interruptions' in the German Romantic poet Hölderlin's poetry, for example, deliberately problematise our ability to 'use' his language as a reader. He says these moments cause language to become conspicuous and 'reveal itself', offering insight into our own state of being in relation to it (Heidegger 2000 [1986], 6). In effect, the existential 'involved enquiry' instigated by the *un*-ready-to-hand tool is replicated in the un-ready language of broken poetry.

Moreover, as David Nowell Smith (2013) has written of Heidegger, it is precisely at the points his readings attempt to describe the brokenness of Hölderlin's poetry that the philosopher transcends the limits of poetics as a field. Smith classes these limits in two ways: 'On the one hand ... the limit between address and addressee ... On the other ... the limits inhering in its own medium' (Nowell Smith 2013, 89). That is, poetics is generally bounded by its concerns with the limits between audiences and writers, and the limits of what language itself is, but Heidegger and Agamben both exit these conventional concerns for poetry writing via the exit points of linguistic breakdown. In the moments the rules that govern poetry are broken and poetry becomes other than itself, poetics also expands as a possibility and can become more than a study of poetry. In a similar fashion (and we could observe the same of the opportunities Chun takes of system leakage to shift between systems analysis and cultural studies), glitch poetics looks to leave the traditional scope of poetics behind at the moments the language system breaks.

Glitch Momentum

As well as expanding the territory for media and digital poetics, I intend this book to rehabilitate the critical potency of 'glitch' after a period in which it has fallen out of fashion. We have become habituated to glitch's signature aesthetics of pixilation and colour 'blooms', and the criticality of the term has also been lost to the prevalence of its use to describe anything that looks digital. The pixilation, blurrings and static of artistic glitch cultures from a decade or more ago have become part of today's media vernacular. The glitch is used as a paradoxically glossy effect to signify authenticity, expertise and a gritty atmosphere in television programmes. It is deployed as ready-made filters on social media platforms and integrated into the distracted temporalities of today's pop music. The result is an accelerated example of the seemingly inevitable fate of avant-garde techniques: as soon they reach a certain level of saturation, they form part of the texture of the mainstream to which they were initially opposed.

Accordingly, critics might observe that this book is naïve, or that it seeks to mainstream a marginal literary practice by hooking it onto a popular vernacular term. But, on the contrary, I take up some more patient, unfashionable tasks. Throughout the book, I am keen to see what theories and practices do when put into combinations not previously tested. For example, Fredric Jameson's ideas on demystification and defamiliarisation in the histories of literary realism (2012) have not been understood through the modalities of new media art or the digital subject (Goriunova 2018). Adorno and Benjamin's works on stasis and cognition in art concerning politics have not, that I know of, been deployed in understanding literature in the context of digital image noise or the coding conventions that contemporary poets write into. Certainly, Menkman's theories around glitch have not been extended into conversation with the theories of contemporary literature that her artistic writing on media vernaculars evokes.[14]

The death of glitch has been announced on several occasions. In art theory, there is a tendency, induced by institutions of finance and status, to promote the death of things prematurely. Indeed, perhaps there is a correspondence here between the way art theory 'tools' are newly minted, developed and dropped, and how 'new media' devices, fashions and trends disrupt and habituate us to their hegemonies of knowledge: an ideology of 'newness' which generates industry noise and little else, and which contradicts what I see as the specific possibility of the glitch as a messy moment that extends, through contemplation and analysis, into a new formulation of what can be done. The anachronistic quality of reading poetry through ideas associated with computers and code is part of its potency, as is the act of re-reading the literature we have been habituated to understanding in a historical light as an exemplar of what is new.

In recent years there has been a flush of theorists revisiting the term 'glitch' for a post-pixel situation. In *Glitch Feminism*, Legacy Russell (2020) takes up the glitch from the perspective of the social outsider who finds themselves at home within cyberculture, where various roles, virtual bodies and identities can be experimented with in ways that illustrate the ways social norms constrain our physical bodies and selves. Russell's view is that the glitch is the name for the liberating potentials coded into all kinds of systems: systems of gender and biology, social systems that stratify work and leisure, literary and artistic systems of privilege and hierarchy

– all containing the possibility of glitches that would allow us to work outside or beyond them. Russell says that the notion of wrongness in technological glitches can be transponded into the forms of 'non-performance' by non-binary individuals in relation to social norms and physical bodies. Being perceived as an error, in this view, is a positive development, allowing one to move outside of the system as well as articulate its limits: 'This failure to function within the confines of a society that fails us is a pointed and necessary refusal. Glitch feminism dissents, pushes back against capitalism' (Russell 2020, 12). Russell's is also a language-glitch deployed as a politic: as a non-binary person who has transitioned from male to female, Russell's glitch feminism concept, by 'refus[ing] to be hewn to the hegemonic line of a binary body', glitches 'feminism' itself, seeking a field of effects within this field by pushing it to mean what she needs. *Glitch Feminism* is an original addition to the field of glitch studies because it bridges the 'digital native's' knowledge of the glitch as a continual, sometimes frustrating, sometimes beautiful, often banal, presence within computational systems with a rising form of identity politics that sees political potential in performances, statements and artistic gestures that work outside of normative constructs. The vectors opened by the glitch do not always accord with the politics of Russell's manifesto, though. Russell's allies within queer and feminist cultures are not the only ones to glitch the social norms and media flows she highlights: the far-right also have made considerable political ground in recent years by working in selective ways outside of accepted behavioural patterns. Nevertheless, her perspective is clear: from the point of view of an individual who is silenced, marginalised and refused status within today's society, new roles and languages, system-altering, system-breaking or exit codes (perhaps rehearsed within the subcultures of the cyberworld) clearly have a particular attraction.

Luciana Parisi and Stamatia Portanova (2011) invite us to consider that the glitch's dominance in artistic discourses around the 'aesthetic of code' has led to a pretty limited discussion around how codes have aestheticised and ruptured thinking in different disciplines. For Parisi, the term 'soft thought' can be used as an alternate route for understanding 'algorithmic or quantitative ideas' as inherently open, and as containing indeterminacies and randomness that do not require the glitch to aestheticise or reveal them. This is an idea I explore in this book through notions such as the 'clean glitch' (Emerson, 2012). To evoke the glitch at each moment the digital reveals itself is reductive in Parisi's view. She coins the term 'soft thought' to articulate the mode of inhuman relation where complex, unpredictable patterns emerge directly from working algorithmic modes of computation. Parisi suggests, like Berry, that 'the acceleration of automation ... invades the everyday', but where her work diverges from notions of a 'glitch ontology' is that Parisi asserts the 'alien reasoning of patternless algorithms' that are inherent in computation without necessarily connecting them to error. In the next-generation technologies Parisi writes about (i.e., mainly AI-assisted architectural design software), the randomness of the glitch becomes a method, like quantification, that underpins the aesthetics of the digital. In this case, we may misrecognise the creative mode of the algorithm's soft thought interaction with material properties as an error, when in fact, 'instead of deriving dynamic patterns of information from matter, patternless data are instead generated within computation itself, and [have become] intrinsic to automated reason' (Parisi 2014, 417). In positing soft thought as an alternative mode by which algorithms can be programmed to push outside of preprogrammed patterns, Parisi is naming the aesthetic possibilities of coded materials that do not require an 'error fetish' to reveal them. While the present book certainly has an error fetish, Parisi's work on soft thought notion also resonates with my impressions of code-influenced contemporary literature that moves beyond 'corrupted' or 'dirty' aesthetics.

Drawing on Parisi's work, Betti Marenko (2015) notes that the 'glitch-event' is the manifestation of an algorithm's 'unknown ability' in its soft thought mode. In this sense, an algorithmic glitch is still a form of unknowing: a 'machine's own incomprehensible, nonhuman thought' manifests itself as a glitch because it reaches outside normalised determinations. Marenko suggests that it is both the 'incomprehensible' capacity of algorithms to produce differentiating outputs *and* the incomprehensibly surprising event of the error that contain potentials for creative production. Often it is impossible to distinguish between the two, primarily because algorithms currently operate with data and materials at vastly larger scales than we can ourselves ever know. In particular, perhaps echoing Russell's utopian approach to the glitch as a concept (and the esoteric traditions of language magic), Marenko is interested in the ways that glitches project into the future: 'It is precisely its location at the boundary between the known and the unknown that turns the glitch into a divining practice' (Marenko 2015, 117).[15] These vectors for thinking the glitch have pushed my own, as I have sought to apply the set of theories coming from 2000s glitch art to literary contexts. Where I accord with Russell, Parisi and Marenko is that the possibility of glitch*ing* is ubiquitous in creative and social spheres, and this requires us to reassess glitch's theoretical use in various fields.

Summary

Formally, a glitch is a revealing error. It is characterised by the qualities of a process layer (code, electronic flows) becoming available in an output layer (images, screens, hardware devices) in the form of breakage or distortion. In a more profound sense, a glitch reveals a complex multi-layering and interaction of the structures and processing errors it has itself broken: process layers can be glitched by breaking the structures that underpin them. Beneath those structures there are process mistakes that may be the 'original' source of the disruption, but the order of this is obscured by the temporally and spatially compressed envelope of digital technology. Glitch poetics is the literary overlaying and entangling of language, readers and writers in the movement of the digital-born error between reception and transmission.

In contradiction to the vernacular use of glitch (as a *hitch*) but in correspondence with the artistic deployment of glitch as a tactic, there is no particular need for the broken text or the broken language logics to be the result of an accident in the writing process. The author is part of a system of layered structures and processes in which disruptions, interventions, distortions and accidents continually appear and are suppressed. Glitchiness, as we have seen, is the product of code languages and 'lower-level' technics administering an inherently unruly balance of material and symbolic inputs. Glitch artists are engaged in various methods for instigating and framing the inherent fragility of the digital system. Glitch poetics writers let the fine-grained entanglement of the human system with the digital into their work as forms of error. Involving and emphasising the writing system's bodily, cognitive and technical complexes, they deploy different kinds of error as allegorical and sensuous tactics. The glitches I write about in the further part of the book are often not an intellectual mobilisation of particular digital knowledge as a compositional tactic, nor are they accidental 'slips' on a computer keyboard or corrupted text files. Instead, they result from a writerly 'openness' to the ambient feelings of an era that has become thoroughly infested by the digital as a complex of cultural and technical forms through which error is woven as a connective thread. Glitch poetics is the return of the fundamental glitchiness of code-human relations into a literary and artistic language that has buried it under the slower-moving normative codes of the literary mainstream.

As an artistic heritage and affinity, glitch poetics develops on the critical creative approaches to technology from glitch art and the glitch artists of the 2000s in particular, and it partakes in an ongoing reappraisal of the potency of error. Critical media practice makes original aesthetic and intellectual gestures by interacting in 'wrong' ways with technology. Though the term 'glitch' has become less popularly used in the art world in recent times, the methodology continues to produce fascinating explorations of commercial technology's effects. What I have sought to retain from the pre-existing definitions and theories of the glitch is its temporal specificity: its particular potency for defining an aesthetic quality to phenomena to which it is contemporary. 'Glitch' is a term that has grown out of Yiddish slang and through analogue media cultures, such as radio and television. The explosion in its use in the last two decades indicates its particular nativity to digital technologies. Still, a human-language version of this phenomenon is not so strange, especially when we consider how, as a result of the increasing use of computers to model, measure and engineer experimental situations, the term has also proliferated among disciplines as diverse as neuroscience and astrophysics, gaming, finance and political analysis. Glitch poetics readings offer a particular opportunity to explore human entanglement with media, using literature as an exemplary unit where human and media errors intersect.

Chapter summaries

The remaining analysis unfolds across three chapters, each of which portrays a particular kind of glitch poetics, respectively addressing the glitch as it exists in performance writing, lyric poetry and realist fiction.

In chapter 1: Body-System Glitch, I look to the blend of art, media, performance and poetry practices called 'performance writing' to explore *glitchfrastructures* (Berlant 2016). These are structures created by artistic errors in language by producing errors in writing and reading systems that reconnect writing and reading bodies to texts in extreme and unusual ways. The chapter is formally unconventional in that, like a code that oscillates between failure and functionality, I frequently switch my focus and mode of analysis. The chapter cuts between close- and through-readings of literary and artistic works, taking in analyses of contemporary and historical media devices, as well as commentary on their social and psychological impacts. Here I illustrate a common trend of evolution, breakage, innovation and habituation that characterises the linguistic avant-garde and the commercial media sphere alike. I also point at instances when these realms overlap and intersect in moments of error. This is important because it means that the glitch in literature presents a critical and aesthetic possibility that reaches outside of literature, a quality that is inherent in the works I analyse in this chapter. Anticipating the 'proto-media realism' concept of the final chapter here, I suggest that glitches, rather than being purely technical or purely experiential phenomena, are best understood as moments in which machinic and cognitive systems are fused into new, futuristic proximities, anticipating the more proximate human-technology relations of a post-human future.

To illustrate the theory of glitch poetics, I perform literary readings of work by Caroline Bergvall and Erica Scourti, showing their resonance and entanglement with new media devices such as the speed reader and predictive text. Bergvall and Scourti are two innovative language practitioners who are rarely written about together, although they collaborated early in Scourti's career. Their work shares a conceptual clarity about language's relation to technology, which makes them excellent examples for media analysis. I use this affinity to structure a reading of four of their key works alongside analysis of specific media devices. Scourti's practice in particular foregrounds how language emerges from today's digital writing and reading tools. Through close working with specific devices, such as the iPhone or Spreeder app, Scourti's work echoes Menkman's by suggesting that such technologies are embedded in our thoughts and actions in a comparable way to a given 'native' vernacular. Glitch poetics offer a mode for reading the textures of error in Scourti's language works, showing how they act as points of emotional and intellectual purchase for their audience. Bergvall's oeuvre has less frequently addressed itself specifically to digital technologies, but I argue that her commitment to viewing language as a politically and historically specific effect has produced several artworks that eloquently communicate the stakes of our intimacy with ever more complex writing devices. I use the framework of glitch poetics to analyse the specific nature of the textual errors in Bergvall's work and relate this analysis to the qualities of wrongness we encounter in contemporaneous technologies.

In chapter 2: Lyric-Code Glitch, I perform close readings of Ben Lerner's *Mean Free Path* (2010) and Keston Sutherland's *The Odes to TL61P* (2013) as examples of contemporary lyrics that negatively figure the digital in relation to the contemporary subject. I read these poems as post-digital works whose concerns spread out from literature to form essential critiques of the temporalities and rhythms of digital media. As in chapter 1, I interpose the literary readings in chapter 2 with analyses of the media apparatus, but in chapter 2, I draw more heavily on studies (or archaeologies) of media and software to illustrate the degree to which glitch poetics transcend the specific knowledge of the practicing poet, and instead render media qualities based on a felt intuition. It is the internalised, habituated version of media that these poets are writing about in their glitchy works. This means there is a resonance between the forms of error in the poems and the mechanisms that underpin how computers work. N. Katherine Hayles has gone as far as stating that 'code is the new unconscious of language' (2006, 136). In Lerner's and Sutherland's work, the linguistic slip and corruption therefore present an interpretable surface texture on which this unconscious can be detected as a trace, echoing the role of error in parapraxis or dream interpretation in psychoanalysis. Sutherland and Lerner consider this to be a technique with political potency – a form of error in which ideological resistance to dominant machinic conditions can illustrate exit points from their grasp.

A Freudian adaptation of Marxist 'praxis' is in tune with Lerner's and Sutherland's affinities with Walter Benjamin and Theodor Adorno, respectively. I show that these affinities can be used to examine the radical shift in the kind of lyric that results from poets opening themselves up to contemporary conditions in the eras of modernity and the digital age. The formal adaptations Lerner and Sutherland apply to the lyric, I suggest, 'negatively figure' the human experiences of the digital age. The way Lerner and Sutherland write is designed as a response to the depth to which algorithmic and micro-archival conditions of digital capitalism have penetrated the contemporary subject: as Lerner says, 'You can't write anything that isn't shot through with capital' (Lerner in Clune 2016). However, as with the genealogy of Adorno and Benjamin's immanent critique, the poets also consider the digital as a site where the contradictions of capitalism are at their most dense, and therefore, by writing through and revealing these contradictions, the poems are pitched as politically active interventions. The chapter develops on the notion of glitch poetics from the first chapter's concern with means. It also suggests a way of reading that reveals the paradoxically strange contemporary realisms in these texts, demonstrating how both poems envisage their political potency.

In chapter 3: Proto-Media-Realist Glitch, I give several examples of contemporary prose novels that include the poetics of glitch and that attempt to trace the absence of glitch practices from a particular area of working-class fiction, in correspondence with historical experimental literature and contemporary art practices. The 'autofictions' of novelists such as Sally Rooney and Tao Lin commonly contain tropes that evoke the forms we see in glitching media devices. In their novels, they render the pixelations and blurred edges of digital images as existential conditions for their characters. My interest in this chapter is to connect these stylistically innovative and recognisably contemporary motifs to a lineage of innovation that has typified literary realism since its birth in the nineteenth century, and to contemporary ideas such as Olga Goriunova's notion of the 'digital subject' (2018), while also acknowledging a distinctive latency or gap in the literary rendering of media intensity. This final chapter aims to draw together my uses of the term 'realism' throughout this book: as innovative, surprisingly recognisable linguistic styles, and hypersensitivities to media environments and where they are heading, but also to the intent to represent people lower in the social strata. The realism of authors from Honoré de Balzac to David Peace concentrates on depicting social forces as they converge on individual bodies. I am interested in the interchangeability of understandings of 'media' with those of 'social forces' today and in how media relations and properness intersect to produce (and fail to produce) errant kinds of literature and art practice with language. A consideration of glitch as realism, I suggest, can also be used to short-circuit the distinction between experimental and literary fiction, and it can return an idea of difficult language to the possibilities of what is sayable about today's working conditions.

Chapter 1

Body-System Glitch

There are two fundamental observations I want to make about language glitches. Firstly, glitches humanise systems: happenstance crashes, unexplained behaviours and even randomness cause us to attribute our computers with a personality of sorts. Secondly, glitches systematise humans, demanding that we acknowledge the complex interrelations of corporeal and conceptual matter at work when we speak or write. Friedrich Kittler (1999) suggests that it is in the figure of the injured body talking gibberish on a hospital bed that the conditions for computational language machines are produced:

> Nature, the most pitiless experimenter, paralyses certain parts of the brain through strokes and bullet wounds to the head: research (since the Battle of Solferino in 1859) is only required to measure the resulting interferences. ... Sensory aphasia (while hearing), dyslexia (while reading), expressive aphasia (while speaking), agraphia (while writing) *bring forth machines in the brain*. (Kittler 1999, 189, emphasis mine)

The textures of error audible in the speech of the aphasic are a rendering of the previously unseen, unknowable language systems of the patient: the mastery of muscular movements in the face, throat and chest; sub-liminal electrical impulses in the brain; the vanishing knowledge of abstract concepts, grammars and meanings. Errors in the human body reveal that language is *only* the manifestation of a system, giving birth to language-making systems such as typewriters and computers: 'When ... language works as a feedback loop of mechanical relays, the construction of typewriters is only a matter of course' (Kittler 1999, 190). For Kittler, ballistic wars intervene in the human body to the extent that they cut right through it. The human, once breached, not only becomes visible as a system of organic and non-organic entities but is also blown apart, de-centred from 'discourse channel conditions' (Kittler 1999, 1), which it now shares with machines. In this chapter, I examine injuries, cuts, and tears in languages, machines and bodies in the work of two performance writers. The glitches we encounter in the form of disruptive new media and in linguistic error, I will show, both present an encounter with a range of systems that cross human bodies and media – and that produce new possibilities for how we conceptualise them.

Posthumanities

Reading computation, biology, history and literature across one another in the glitch is a form of posthumanities: a field that emerges from the numerous pressures on the integrity of 'the human' as rendered in humanist discourse, breaking open the silo between arts and sciences subjects. In her book *The Posthuman* (2013), Rosi Braidotti outlines feminist, postcolonial and antiracist politics as inaugurating the dispersal of the Enlightenment figure of 'man' (and specifically, the white European man) as the 'measure of all things' (Braidotti 2013, 13). Braidotti draws into this emphasis on the politics of difference more recent ruptures, such as big data and artificial intelligence, and the seismic environmental events that have led scientists to coin the term 'the Anthropocene' (Waters *et al.* 2018). Each of these ruptures in the established norms that produced 'the human' entity, Braidotti argues, breaches the distinctions between human/machine, human/earth and human/animal, to the degree that the category of 'the human' itself becomes difficult to uphold: glitching it outward into its technical and ecological environment. The convergence of these pressures on the boundary project of the human – and therefore the humanities as a field of study – establishes an environment in which we must now seriously consider the posthuman as *the* category for sciences, arts and media.

In *The Posthuman Glossary*, Braidotti and Maria Hlavajava suggest that there is 'the emergence of a transdisciplinary discourse that is more than the sum of posthumanism and post-anthropocentrism, and points to a qualitative leap in a new – perhaps 'post-disciplinary' – critical direction' (Braidotti and Maria Hlavajava 2018, 4). Notably, Braidotti and Hlavajava also suggest that the posthuman moment requires its own language: 'As the "Generation Anthropocene" we believe that new notions and terms are needed to address the constituencies and configurations of the present and to map future directions' (1). This is a moment, the authors suggest, characterised by pressures, fissures and reconfigurations, where the conclusions we draw from spikes in ecological data are enmeshed with 'the changes induced by advanced technological developments on the one hand and the structural inequalities of the neoliberal economics of global capitalism on the other' (1). The focus of Braidotti and Hlavajava is less on the new geological epoch than on the glitchy, system-altering exceptions – including those in language – that accompany its effects.

Glitch theory is post-disciplinary: along with media and literary examples, biomedicine has traditionally relied on linking systematically 'wrong' behaviours to structural injury in order to draw conclusions regarding how the body works. Genetics scientists inaugurate glitches in DNA structures to diverge from current species categories, creating new human-animal or super-human cell formations. The human impact on the Earth's atmosphere presents to us as a series of glitches in climate and geological data: the tragic anomalous events such as the 2019 Australian bush fires, the 2020 flash floods in Afghanistan or the ongoing famine in Yemen.[16] Contemporary discourse is also characterised by vernacular anomalies, the texture of which are testimony to the blending of worlds and world views in the post-disciplinary condition. The glitch poetics events I will discuss in this chapter are moments in which the body system lives through new links between its biological mass and the machinic systems around it. The nature of the new and like-new systems that emerge in the moment of error can be first detected in the terminologies they demand around them: fragile slang and forms of incoherence, which give way to new norms and understandings.

Glitchfrastructure

In her work on the commons, Lauren Berlant has referred to the Occupy protest camp in New York using the neologism 'glitchfrastucture' (Berlant 2016, 396). For Berlant, the camp's systems of communication and administration are productively unstable. The concentration of erratic, errant activity in the camp interferes with the systems that normally codify behaviour in the public spaces it occupies and govern the urban administrative apparatus around and across them. The errors in the camp-system are themselves proto-systems that demand new kinds of response from the city-system. Berlant's glitchy portmanteau signifies (and performs) a disruption with constructive, or rather restructuring, potentials.

Infrastructures are different to systems because 'infrastructure is defined by the movement or patterning of social form. It is the living mediation of what organises life: the lifeworld of structure' (Berlant 2016, 394). The city's infrastructure is a 'living mediation' between the people who live there and the laws that govern them, and the glitchfrastructure also lives, re-breeding the city's structures from within, albeit temporarily. Misbehaviour becomes a glitchfrastructure when it is sustained, and forces flows (of traffic, people, information, goods, vernacular) to reshape themselves around it, like a habit that absorbs disruptive technology and turns it into social norms.

For now, I want to appropriate *glitchfrastructure* as a make-do name for what is created when a reader encounters a literary error, and the cognitive and physical components of their reading 'infrastructure' are rerouted around it. Literary and para-literary glitchfrastructures open up new possibilities for a text to network readers and authors. The anomalous activity in a textual glitch is a kind of proto-convention, potentially 'generating a form from within brokenness beyond the exigencies of the current crisis' (Berlant 2016, 394)[17] into new modes for language practice.

Human and nonhuman systems in crisis, broken bodies and broken texts, troubled readers and writers reorganise and are reorganised in Erica Scourti and Caroline Bergvall's language works. These artists do not identify themselves as posthuman or, indeed, as glitch artists. Still, their work combines a technical emphasis with themes of new globalised politics and feminist discourse in ways that recall Braidotti's notion of the posthumanities. Their deployment of error and failure as critical aesthetic effects resonates with Menkman's. Through glitch poetics, commercially available 'disruptive technologies', such as speed readers and predictive text, also offer opportunities to restructure a writer's relationship with their audience.

Tactical Media Authorship

In an interview with Scott Thurston in 2011, Caroline Bergvall coined the term 'tactical authorship' to describe her language- and text-based art practice. The range and variety of approaches in Bergvall's oeuvre, she says, is a response to 'technological society [and its]... urban and telematic living', and the diffuse ways that the structures of colonialism are echoed in digital apparatus such as the internet (Thurston 2011, 81). Bergvall suggests that the colonialism infused in today's technologies is 'difficult for literature as an institution to cope with'. Literary forms inherited from modernity, such as the lyric poem or the novel, have become somehow insufficient to the political task at hand. The literary establishment, the publishing and commissioning apparatuses that privilege Anglo-American voices, for example, are also compromised. As a result, we often see in her work an engagement with fringe, para-literary textual practices, performance and publishing methods that problematise the relationship between literary form, cultural platform and media. Bergvall's 'tactical authorship' coinage connects her work to the 'tactical media' field (Raley 2009) in which, Bergvall says, new media artists 'enter, dis-enter, or disinter the public spheres; turning media workings on themselves to circulate other messages' (Thurston 2011,

56). As I will show, this affinity with tactical media is more than a convenient simile. It illustrates Bergvall's awareness of how her work circulates (and intervenes) as a media practice.

In 2009-10, Erica Scourti worked as an assistant on the performance version of Bergvall's *Drift*. By this point, Bergvall was already firmly established as a leading voice in innovative language practice, having helped define the territories of 'performance writing' and the concerns of women's conceptual writing through essays, performances and published works. Scourti was emerging as one of the most prominent of a generation of media artists who use language performance as a way of exploring our increasing intimacy with social media and mobile technology. The working relationship between Bergvall and Scourti suggests a critical affinity that reaches across a generational and disciplinary divide. It is the affinity between Bergvall and Scourti's approaches to language-as-media and media-of-language respectively, approaches that the concept of glitch poetics draws out. Glitch poetics, after all, is a name for a principle in which media-language practices redraw the boundaries that distinguish texts and technologies, and individual and social bodies.

About Face

'About Face' is Bergvall's most evidently glitchy text. The poem is a transcription of sorts. She describes the occasion that marks and scores the text: 'An infected tooth had been extracted prior to leaving London. The sutured pain and phantom bone made it difficult to articulate the text to the audience' (Bergvall 2005, 33). The written version of the poem Bergvall attempted to perform is published in her book *Fig* (2005), where the difficulty in articulating the script is folded back into the surface of the poem as textual aposiopesis, repetitions, jumbling of letters and other disfluencies. Examining this work's process forces us to consider the contradictory view that our jaw, while being 'us', is also an 'external' we *use* when we speak, and so is prone to malfunction. As Bergvall asserts, 'speech fluency is an articulatory feat... It presupposes the smooth functioning of speaking's motor skills. It is a choreography of the physiological mouth into language' (2005, 33).

The patterns of Bergvall's wounded jaw performance are added to in the text of the 'About Face' poem, along with layer artefacts from recording, transcribing and speaking. Each layer is articulated as errors. The final poem also includes fragments of a conversation between Redell Olsen and Bergvall recorded on minidisc before being transcribed and integrated into the text. The poem and interview are 'written into' by minidisc edits and the stop-start mechanism of the recording device. The stumbles and disorders of the glitchy vocal delivery resulting from Bergvall's wounded jaw are combined and compounded with the cuts and splices of the minidisc, and the hesitations and disfluencies of 'everyday speech', laminated into the final text. 'This isn't all about teeth ... micro-frictions from this live language were added to the written text' (33).

We encounter the glitches of technology (minidisc), the human technics (tooth, jaw) and other operations (transcription, listening), flattened together as an increasingly disorderly misplacement of letters and words, where the act of mediating the text predominates over what the text says. Bergvall chooses to retain many of the recognisable aspects of the poem form: 'About Face' is linear and reads in horizontal lines that are ordered in a list down the page, unlike Marinetti's futurist works or Steve McCaffery's 'dirty concrete' poems, for example. But a close reading reveals increasingly severe disorders within these parameters, each of which equates to a given 'messy media moment', an error resulting from a malfunction in the jaw or minidisc, or a mistake made in transcription. The disorders in the early parts of the poem evoke the slurs and stammers of someone having trouble speaking:

> This is not a face
>
> a f s a face is like a rose
>
> s easier l this
>
> th n fss
>
> correlated to ah yes tt t waltzing (45)

The later disorders, sometimes using line breaks, suggest the sharp cuts of a recording device being turned on and off during the recording: 'Motion sparks nameless noise and the others are diff / walking up to taking turn' (43). As it progresses, the poem overlays different kinds of textual glitch with such frequency that they cannot be distinguished from one another. Despite the intensity of these ruptures, we feel how the 'original' utterance has been altered by the process of transmission. To take a particular example: 'a f s a face is like a rose / s easier I this / th n fss correlated to ah yes tt t waltzing t change' (35). There are numerous types of media error here, but they are difficult to separate from the errant quality of language in a poem. Perhaps the original version of this extract was *a face, a face is like a rose / is easier in this / than a face correlated to waltzing to change*. The repetition in the first line could be a vocal stammer or a reference to a 1922 Gertrude Stein line, 'a rose is a rose is a rose'. The capital 'I' in the second line is almost certainly a computer auto-correct, mis-correcting the misspelling of 'in'. '[T]h n fss' could be a vocal slurring of *than a face*. '[A]h yes tt t' is perhaps an interruption from the conversation with Olsen, followed by some 'tt t' disc-edit artefacts, which could also be tongue-stumbles. The final phrase is syntactically wrong; perhaps words lost between *correlated to* and *waltzing to,* or *correlated to waltzing and,* but combined (or correlated) with the word 'waltzing'. It could be that the syntax slippage is deliberate and 'waltzing to change' is being treated as a noun.

Indeed, the types of error in 'About Face' provide clues to decoding an original or a set of original sources. Still, these also lead us elsewhere, towards the events of transmission that have taken place between Bergvall and us. The glitches in the text operate as signs for the times and processes that separate us from Bergvall's 'original' performance in New York, offering a gappy, productively ambiguous picture of this process. 'About Face' uses the radically simplified constraint of the text to entangle human and machinic slips with poetic technique as a single interference pattern. As multiple puns available in its title suggest, this is an incredibly efficient work, using the ambiguity of error to combine several layers of articulation in it. We oscillate, or 'about face' between the 'abouting' of faces: Bergvall's face, Olsen's and Bergvall's face-to-face, the inter-face of the minidisc, the sur-face of the text; each manifest and emphasise themselves in the text and, in turn (as I show below), the work becomes about our faces also.

The wit of 'About Face' recalls another recording-device work made around the same time. Janek Schaffer's *Recorded Delivery* (1995) was created by boxing up a sound-activated tape recorder and posting it from Exhibition Road in Central London, near the artist's studio, to a self-storage site ten miles away. The tape recorder automatically excerpted the 15-hour journey with the postal service to a 72-minute recording, capturing just 'the most sonically interesting elements' of the journey. Listening to the work, we hear voices in snatches that are obscured by zips, the jostling movement of the bag, the ironic jokes and slogans repeated by staff in the sorting office performing for each other, immediately followed by car doors slamming, sorting office machines. As with Bergvall's poem, the human voices encountered are conjoined with the mechanics of the journey between the origin and the final work, and the internal workings of the device used to record it.

Bergvall's poem in its written form is silent but 'sonically interesting'. It invites us to perform it, if only under our breath. When we read this work, language, at once physiological, technological and typographical, becomes evident in our own bodies: gaps in the text open gasps in our chest, slowing and emphasising our eyes' and minds' engagement with letter-ordering. Our reading struggle is an echo of Bergvall's vocal stutter, or the clack of a minidisc button. That is to say, when we read 'About Face' the body is decoding the manifest errors in the poem, playing it back.

The process of embodiment as we play a poem back silently while reading is called subvocalisation. Garrett Stewart describes subvocalisation as 'the role of silent reading as the internalisation of literate consciousness' (2015, 61). It is an involuntary muscular response to reading text, by which letters registered by the visual cortex simulate a kind of ghost movement in our vocal cords and tongue. The role of subvocalisation is amplified and problematised by Bergvall's emphasis on the stammer in 'About Face'. This is to say, in 'About Face', the range of errors – Bergvall's struggle with her jaw, the struggle of transcription to contain conversation, the minidisc edit – are given additional 'volume' inside the skull and throat of the reader, because they are hard for us to articulate: the corrupted text becomes difficult to swallow (or is it 'bring up'?), and therefore noteworthy.

This formal emphasis on the technics connecting our throat to our cognitive capacities resonates with the poem's themes. The subvocalisation of 'About Face' is a glitchfrastructure as sensual hermeneutics: an empathic tissue where we are reconnected to Bergvall's inability to speak in a New York poetry reading, to conversations she had with Redell Olsen, and where we are taken inside the mechanical and magnetic workings of a minidisc. Subvocalisation is a valuable concept for glitch poetics because it offers a way of explaining how the glitch in a text gains purchase on the body, becoming a lived, felt experience as it is read and understood. Still, the critical and sensory qualities of text can also be combined in language error by the absence of physicality. Here, we can turn to speed readers.

Speed Readers

Speed reader apps use rapid serial visual presentation (RSVP), showing texts a word at a time at frequencies of up to 700 words per minute, suppressing subvocalisation. The first proto-speed reader was a mechanical projection device proposed by the artist Bob Brown in the 1930s. Brown described it as a 'simple reading machine which I can carry or move around, attach to any old electric light plug and read hundred thousand word novels in ten minutes if I want to, and I want to' (Brown 1930, 28). Brown's innovation formally departed from the book, not only because it replaced the lineated, multi-word page with single-word, rapid and serial presentations, but also because the words themselves took the 'form of light'. Brown said reading his machine texts was 'more akin to [them] beaming onto the eye, rather than the solid printed word' (Thomas 2012). The same technique of showing words in quick succession using light is used in software applications that run on commonly available smartphones or computer screens.

The rapidity of RSVP means that our bodies subdue the subvocalisation mechanism and eye saccades (back-and-forth eye movements required by horizontal line reading) that are usually part of the reading system. Companies making RSVP commercially available as a digital service, such as Spritz, claim that the microscopic movements of the eye and throat muscles are a waste of time (Spritzinc.com 2016). Instead, the vaporous light-text becomes 'more efficient' by bypassing specific bodily processes. We might now 'inhale the text', Spritz suggests. RSVP software imagines that the eye and throat mechanisms of reading are extraneous. They deconstruct the bodily apparatus in posthuman fashion, positing eye muscles and vocal cords as 'unnatural' supplements to the *necessary* technics of recognising and processing text quickly. Speed readers produce a glitchfrastructure in the reading system, pulling out some aspects of the system and temporarily reorganising the body and mind around them. The 'new natural' of a muscle-free reading offers itself as an inverse kind of glitch to the overload of mouth-technics marking Bergvall's 'About Face'.

When I encounter a speed reader text displaying white words, one word at a time, on a black screen, I experience a phenomenological confusion: I am reading, then, almost imperceptibly, I appear to be falling or travelling among lines ... then thoughts. Is this text happening to me, rather than me happening to it? The encounter with speed readers has a destabilising quality – the uncanniness associated with early experiences of glitch – but rather than the shock of *too much* sensuality, there is a feeling of *vertigo,* weightlessness, sensory deprivation. Following this kind of logic, media archaeologist Lori Emerson (2014, 40) describes a recent speed reader electronic literature work by Young Hae Chang Heavy Industries (YHCHI) as 'clean glitch'. This artist-duo's works do indeed look clean, almost sleek, as they play out on our screens, using a single monochrome and monospace typeface, a word at a time, synchronised with a snappy jazz soundtrack.

Emerson's separation of glitchiness from the aesthetics and textures of corruption emphasise the artwork's critical reception, the cut it makes in our aesthetic sensibility and the way it provokes the bodily systems adapted to reading and browsing on screens. All new media devices and language artefacts, regardless of their glitchy appearances, have the potential to challenge and stop us in this manner, asking us to think again and reconnecting our normative behaviour in new ways. For Emerson, the glitch in YHCHI's work is not the suppression of subvocalisation, but rather another lack. The 'utter lack of interactivity' in 'Break Down the Doors' constitutes a significant break with the new normal of screen-based experiences premised on clickables, scrolls and movable windows; therefore, she says, we encounter the work as a glitch in our everyday flow. Normal web-based viewing and reading are characterised by a great deal of interactivity, but YHCHI's non-interactive JavaScript window intrudes on us, occupying our desktops and attention for a set time. It captures us or invites us to refuse it. Importantly, Emerson affirms that this design of difficulty is a critical tool:

> The reader/viewer cannot fast-forward or rewind; they can only click away from the piece and end the experience altogether. YHCHI's dislike of interactivity is also derived from their sense that the Web has become so familiar to us that we're not even aware of its structures, its codes, and the way it works on us rather than us working on it. (Emerson 2014, 41)

This kind of glitch is characteristic of what Menkman has described as glitch artists' will 'to assess the inherent politics of any kind of medium' by forcing a user into a different kind of relation with it (Menkman 2011, 11). In YHCHI's work, the political stubbornness of the web medium productively interacts with the frenetic quality of the words on screen.

The experience of reading RSVP texts and other time-based text works such as YHCHI's pushes against the habits we have developed for reading, producing new critical potentials relating not solely to the interface we see them through but also to our reading capacity. RSVP subdues the components of the reading system that seemed integral to what reading is (such as subvocalisation and eye saccades) in a way that is analogous to a full-screen window obscuring our online-clickables; but the pressures relieved from the throat and mouth interactions of subvocalisation push back into the body, causing formerly subdued aspects of the reading system, such as blink reflexes and iris contractions, to permeate our experience of the text.

YHCHI's media poems and Bob Brown's poem-machines are sites where innovative poetics induce problems and difficulties in existing systems, using a technique that will later form the basis of a 'disruptive' consumer device. The avant-garde frequently problematises media systems in ways that are fully compatible with commercial culture's need to continually redraw its sphere of influence (an affinity that is perhaps ironically gestured towards by YHCHI's presentation of themselves as a 'heavy industries company' rather than an artist partnership). A reading of the politics of disruptive media practices must be emphatically contextual for this reason.

Poetry and the Semio-economy

The proximity between the avant-garde breakdown of technical norms, and commercial cultures' lust for innovation and efficiency requires a close reading that links form, content and intent. Post-Marxist thinkers such as Franco Berardi (2012) have levelled convincing critiques towards the media environments of the most recent brands of capitalist innovation, illustrating especially how such environments connect to abusive cognitive labour conditions, which seem to be embodied in speed readers' acceleration of the clickable screen (notwithstanding the labour conditions in the countries that produce the hardware which digital tech relies on). Berardi uses the term 'semiocapitalism' to refer to the 'new regime characterised by the fusion of media and capital', suggesting that '[i]n this sphere, poetry meets advertising and scientific thought meets the enterprise' (Berardi 2009, 18). In *Poetry and Finance* (2012), he dates the rupture in media and capital flows that result in today's semiocapital conditions to the activity of the avant-garde before the electronic revolution, making a connection between nascent financial markets and the symbolist poetry of the nineteenth century.

Berardi suggests that the separation of referential 'words' from the world of denoted 'things' by symbolists' radical wordplay created a situation where language came to be notionally infinite, existing on a different plane from material contingencies of the world:

> The experience of French and Russian symbolism broke the referential-denotative between the word and the world. At the same time, Symbolist poets enhanced the connotational potency of language to the point of explosion and hyperinclusion. Words became polysemous evocations for other words, and thus became epiphanic. (Berardi 2012, 18)

'Epiphanic' here refers to language that invokes itself directly into a person's knowledge: making an image, deity or world appear 'from nothing'. The epiphany, like speed reading, elides the physical infrastructure of reading by implying a lossless transmission for a poetic image that 'explodes' in the mind. Later in this same text, Berardi is more equivocal about the relation between symbolist poetry and the move towards the semio-economy, suggesting the 'magic of postreferential language *anticipated* the general process of dereferentialisation that occurred when the economy became a semio-economy' (Berardi 2012, 18-19 emphasis mine). Symbolists either anticipated or invented the financial industry by glitching language away from meaning. The poetic token of the epiphanic word – originally an emancipatory gesture – was alighted on and accelerated as a logic for an economy based on trade freed from material consequences.

Like epiphanic language, the semio-economy contains in it an ideal for exchange in which value is summoned without material friction: semiocapital directly appropriates what it perceives as an excess capacity of the human, analogous to the poetic inference that exceeds the referential meaning of words and absorbs it into its value system. The emblematic inventions of the semio-economy are those that allow for the direct financialisation of 'immaterial' activity while subduing the role of the materials on which they rely; in the same way as Spritz's invention claims to transcend the eye saccade and throat twitch, manual labour is considered too slow for the newer, sleeker form of profit making. The digital products that Silicon Valley companies such as Facebook, Google, eBay and Uber trade in are centrally concerned with monetising the moment of exchange while bracketing the labour and environmental price, and avoiding public taxation.[18] Kennedy and Zysman (2016) draw attention to how these kinds of companies intervene in and 'disrupt' existing, physical exchange relationships, producing new movements of information in order to extract additional financial value from the relative rapidity and scale available when executing transactions in this way. 'Disruptive' platforms such as Uber replicate the dematerialising tendency of financial stock-markets, where named company stocks are bought and sold in a manner – and at a speed – that disregards the nature and consequences of the company's actual business practice, at the level of the human. The exclusion of material products, consequences and bodies from the spreadsheets of businesses, Berardi suggests, contributes to a culture that valorises the limitless acceleration over the effects realised at the ground zero of the physical body.

Berardi's polemic calls for a return to the material concerns of poetry and finance, centring on the case of the Greek economic crisis, during which people have been increasingly subject to material privation in the name of servicing an irredeemable 'abstract' debt. He suggests that the way this situation has played out under the ideological instruction of financial institutions illustrates an acute disregard for bodies:

> The financial class which has taken the reins of the European political machine has no attachment either to territory or to material production, because its power and wealth are founded on the total abstraction of digital finance. This

> digital-financial hyperabstraction is liquidating the living body of the planet and the social body of the workers' communities. … [T]he global mind went crazy because individual brains and individual bodies are not capable of limitlessly going faster and faster and faster. (Berardi 2012, 114)

The suppression of subvocalisation and eye mechanisms by speed readers and the invocation companies such as Spritz make of the accelerate-able cognitive potentials of their users turn speed readers into a symptomatic example of the semiocapitalist disregard for what bodies are capable of, especially as it unfolds from poetic (and glitch poetic) practice. However, as I have suggested above, it does not take long when using speed readers to experience something of their maddening and somewhat physical effects. So it is also worth asking: can the speed reader-induced glitchfrastructure also produce *more powerful* sensual encounters between bodies and texts, offering a critical new interaction gestalt for poetry and the cognitive economy?

By connecting a glitch poetics reading of Bergvall's 'About Face' to the proposal that speed readers might emphasise some forms of sensuality, even as they suppress others, I want to illustrate the heterogeneous quality of excessive language events. RSVP overflows the economic ideology that it currently operates under by accelerating it, offering a paradoxical material encounter with the ideology of immaterial flows and a mode of purchase for critical and sensory exploration. In the case of the speed reader, it is possible to examine the contradictions between our material encounter with the technology and the ideal use its progenitors espouse – contradictions which are the subject of Erica Scourti's work *Negative Docs* (2015).

Datafication and the Body

An accelerated and amplified intimacy typifies Scourti's work with and through media. Her work is frequently centred around ongoing documentation of her emotional and personal life made on her iPhone and distributed via user-generated content platforms such as YouTube. Scourti uses these popularly available new media devices and platforms in ways that underline the habits they develop in us. Well-known artworks by Scourti with these features include *Body Scan* (2014), in which the artist uses the image-recognition software embedded in Google's search engine 'making literal the objectification of female bodies on the Internet', and a *Life in Adwords* (2012-2013), in which Scourti emailed her diary to herself using Google's email service Gmail and read out the list of products and services that Google's Adwords interface suggested for her.

Much of Scourti's work, as with *Negative Docs* (2015) discussed below, perform the 'datafication' of the human body by exaggerating the artist's involvement with consumer technologies. During a performance at the Sonic Acts Festival in 2017, Scourti spoke of feeling like 'a biology of shock waves crashing on value dis-counters and then statistically having to repeat myself' (Scourti 2017). As with Bergvall, Scourti highlights the political dimensions of our entanglement with media systems:

> It's time you examine yourself and your place in our social, political institutions – including technology which releases all sorts of energies into our lives, so that we become efficient software ... [These] affective interfaces which attempt to tell ... which human emotions can be read with the intention of ending all uncertainty and commercialising it too. (Scourti 2017)

We can characterise Scourti's work as a critique of the 'immaterial' and 'excess' labour notions that are inherent to semiocapitalism. Her artistic text-performances glitch between machine- and human-likeness, and, as a result, also at the brink of what is bearable, as a critique of 'this idea that you can become a better person, or more efficient, this idea that we can become like machines!' (Scourti 2017). It is this tipping point between human and machine, bearable and not, so movingly expressed in Scourti's work, that I will look to draw out in the following readings.

Negative Docs

The 2015 film *Negative Docs* consists of Scourti's diary of the previous year, organised by a semantics-sorting algorithm, so extracts appear in order of increasing emotional negativity. The extracts are played back through a speed reading app, and Scourti reads along until – and after – she loses pace with it. As an accompanying text from the website of the Situations gallery says, the video is 'a performative reading of Scourti's descent into depression and her inability to keep pace with life' (Scourti 2015). Scourti uses the speed reader to unnaturally accelerate her verbal record of depression, and the disruption between what she can say and the excesses of the speed reading software gathers a semiotic meaning within the performance. Our inability to read the speed reader while listening to Scourti's voice textures our encounter with the artist's diaries in a way that signals to us what it is like to live while subject to ever-accelerating semiotic extraction. Importantly, this means the deployment of the speed reader as a metonym for semiocapitalist ideals derives its affective potency from our own struggle. For us as viewers, it is impossible to cope with the gap opening between what we hear and see; the voice that lags and catches on our ear, the text that loses touch with our eyes, the words that spiral into negativity, the machine that ploughs it forward.

Our encounter with the relation between a word as spoken and one as read is a flickering gap that reveals and activates an empathic connection. It rehearses one of the central concerns of the diary's content:

> I've felt very ousted, disconnected, it feels too overwhelming ... just keeps on coming, it is a hard decision, but at least I can have some peace. But ... I can't be everything to everyone and like it or not it means I am always going to be stuck in certain places ... There are always going to be

> battles ... feeling under attack in ways that you cannot control last night character traits like thick house paint ... being at the mercy of other people's whims and desires. (Scourti 2015 [transcription from video])

The error experience of *Negative Docs* pushes the meaning of Scourti's reading beyond the semiotic into a felt experience. As Scourti's voice falls behind the visual display, our brain struggles to broaden its perceptive capacity. The gap opened between the excessive capacity of the speed reading device and the relative incapacitation of Scourti's voice resonates with the gap opening between the excesses of emotional experience and incapacities of language to articulate them: as it gets progressively more negative, Scourti's script becomes more fragmented. This progression produces other tensions: between the disunity of the video's medium specificity and the convention of visual and audio words coinciding;[19] between the different phrases in the work that are reordered by the semantic algorithm; between the words in those phrases that, as they record more difficult mental states, fail to cohere into sentences. These tensions (akin to the oscillations between breakage and function referred to by David Berry [2011]) extend into a moment of discovery. As with Bergvall's 'About Face', our knowledge of the work is determined by how the work's glitches transmit sensations from Scourti's experience to our own. By misusing the speed reading interface, this work subverts what appears to be the speed reader's central ideologies of speed and immateriality, grounding our response in the inherent resistances the body offers to language errors. In this way, the work (perversely, perhaps) constitutes the kind of empathic potential described by Berardi as the sensual excess of poetry: 'the return of the sensuous body of language' (Berardi 2012, 140). It is a work that derives its sensuous possibility by performatively problematising the link between voice and the written word.

Think You Know Me

In another work from this period, Scourti glitches our encounter with human-machine languages by using the iPhone's autocomplete text function. Standing onstage at Transmediale in February 2015, Scourti reads from her telephone screen a kind of autobiographical *dérive*. The words she speaks are unstable in character, oscillating between the banal 'St Andrews street parking directions', intimate 'I guess you could let me down', funny 'look up and see what do the stars say Statistically', incorrect 'appear to the the the the the same', and the kind of art-theory speak one would expect on this stage, 'to create a self-organisation means'. It is seemingly improvised, though the script, simultaneously appearing in a flickering speed reader like text form via an HDMI adaptor connecting her phone to a large screen, could also be a teleprompt. In fact, this work *is* improvised, just not by Scourti herself. The artist is reading directly from auto-suggestions provided by the Evernote app on her iPhone, which has 'learned' to anticipate her based on a legacy corpus of her blog postings, emails, texts, Facebook status updates and tweets. The performance subverts the normative relationship between the spoken word, the speaker and the audience: here, the technology 'performs' a text, outputting it through Scourti's voice. The result is a 'live' text that is uncannily evocative and appropriate to the situation in which it is being read, while also textually and semantically strange.

It is in deviations from what can be said onstage during such a performance, in often humourous glitches in the habitual linguistic norms of the art conference, that we recognise the nature of the technology-disruption to the textual system and the infrastructures that surround it. Paradoxically, this poetic hybrid of intimacy, banality, poetic, intellectual and critical modes, and humour is precisely what we have come to expect from Scourti the artist. As with *Negative Docs,* Scourti's vocal fluency is pushed against the fluency of the machine. Her speech, predisposed towards a particular flow, is pressurised by the excess fluencies of the predictive text technology. The relative speed of her fingers and voice are also measured against the phone's responsiveness. We have a sense, in relation to the patterns of error in Scourti's speech, and visible in the accompanying screen shots (fig. 7), that something is wrong. These patterns are different from the ones in 'About Face', of course, as what is being broken or faltering is code, not a body. Scourti reads quickly, but she does not struggle to keep up; instead, the emphasis is on the kinds of mistake the machine makes in the context of

THINK YOU KNOW ME

Hello my name is live in the UK for a while to reply to your account after the war in the morning of my favourite colour is not the absence of fear in gone to the right to the right place at St Andrews Street parking restrictions on my work and of the blue sky blue sky is the most of the day before the end of this week and I am unable to find the right place for you can see the latest version and then we will try dm and then the Yeah I think the only way we do you want these days and will not t the the the the best way of doing it for the delay i can you please send I love you so much better than this Yeah she's nice I don't know her well as the world seems inexplicably beautiful even tho u know very little time to spare parts for the delay in replying to your account after the war in the UK for the first one is was "Cosmically opaque

Fig. 7. Screenshot from Erica Scourti's 'Think You Know Me, 2015. It shows live predictive text on Scourti's iPhone's keyboard, utilising shortcuts and learnt patterns of text recognition. Transmediale opening ceremony, HKW, Berlin.

the performance event: the breathlessness that emerges largely from the propensity the software has for chaining distinct phrases and clauses without punctuation or pause, 'Can't feel shit Statisically if you see the latest in touch with you I love you so much better after being a version', and the weird semantic leaps it makes, 'who is secretary to the invisible'. This iPhone glitch does not fragment and cut up the text but rather causes syntactical bleeds and splurges, as phrases spill into each other, overflowing the framework of grammatical norms.

The sentences here go on without a particular beginning or end or consequence, evoking the ideals Berardi identifies in semiocapitalist transactions. The punctuation error arises because the iPhone or Evernote software identifies each lexical unit unchained from its context, particularly evident when it uses several vernacular coinages in quick succession: 'time to time and money are safe and sound quality is excellent'. This tendency in the iPhone's native language is put in tension with Scourti's performing body, which falters and pauses over complex or nonsensical lines (although she does admirably in smoothing over these), reminding us that the reading body's ability to voice is linked to the mind's ability to make sense.

There is a political significance to these errors in this work. It links emotional and intellectual capability to the ideologies embedded in the iPhone while reminding us of the leaky intrusions Apple and other Silicon Valley technologies make into our private correspondence as part of their functioning. There is also an archaeological aspect to this work. In the overextended sentences of *Think You Know Me,* we observe the brief moment in history when predictive text used a relatively primitive algorithm, weighting the probability of a word based solely on the previous one. Scourti's rapid, machinic speech in this work marks the horizon of the software's map of language in its 2015 instantiation, before it was updated to the more complex statistical weightings, which perform their predictions at the level of the glyph and therefore include more 'realistic' punctuation and grammar. In this way, Scourti's glitches date the media it uses.

Combinatory and Generative Error

Gertrude Stein's *How to Write* (1931 [1978]) runs through grammatical possibilities for a sentence with a propulsive quality that anticipates the logic (and forms of error) of predictive text.

> Grammar is a conditional expanse. Supposing there is a word let us say predicted and include beyond that color and coloring, prepared to help it will be rapidly dispersed in as many ways that they finally do relish harpoons in a mixed implication that have curtains faults. This is ideally ever ever as well as they can in courage. (Stein 1978, 82)

As the passage above semantically falls apart (somewhere around 'do relish harpoons') or stammers ('ideally ever ever as well'), it puts emphasis not on the semantic flow of the entire paragraph or sentence, but rather on the logic that one word will follow the next. Stein's work is generative (and very much like Scourti's) in the sense that it uses the current word as the sole determining factor for what the next one should be: it follows grammatical rules, but with a short-term memory.

Early computing offers a bridge between experiments such as Stein's and predictive text technology. In 1952, a novice computer scientist called Christopher Strachey used the new computers at Alan Turing's National Research and Development Corporation to devise and run a programme that produced combinatory love letters. In 2012 the artist David Link restaged this work, and he quotes one of the letters on his website:

> HONEY DARLING
>
> MY HEART FONDLY TREASURES YOUR TENDER FELLOW FEELING. MY LOVELY AFFECTION HOPES FOR YOUR FONDNESS. MY LIKING CARES FOR YOUR LOVABLE ENCHANTMENT. MY LOVE EAGERLY CHERISHES YOUR LONGING. MY AFFECTIONATE INFATUATION WISTFULLY LUSTS FOR YOUR YEARNING.
>
> YOURS PASSIONATELY
>
> M. U. C.

Strachey's 'project' was not considered at the time to be part of mainstream innovation: 'Those doing real men's jobs on the computer, concerned with optics or aerodynamics, thought this silly' (Wardrip-Fruin 2011, 312). Nevertheless, similar to Stein's and Scourti's poems, there is a quaintly literary quality to the ways words are connected. Though grammar as a scheme has been necessarily prioritised over the relative meaning of word-units – 'MY LOVELY AFFECTION HOPES FOR YOUR FONDNESS', for example, contains a formula that would work for some word combinations, but here the text's 'affective' quality overburdens its meaning. The effect is disarming, if not believable. The difference between the combinatory, generative literature derived from Strachey's machine and today's predictive text (or chatbots) is that, rather than serving as a discrete database of possibilities, predictive text is – theoretically at least – plugged into a continually updating corpus of 'all possible words', from which it chooses the statistically best, writing the result back into its corpus's map of grammatical likelihoods. Notwithstanding this difference, Strachey's deployment of a random number generator into poetry opens a dialogue that continues between the avant-garde operating at the fringes of literature and technology today, particularly those that experiment with the possibilities of 'believable' and 'recognisable' human-computer collaboration.

Raymond Queneau's *One Hundred Thousand Billion Sonnets*, published in French in 1961, is another touchstone work in the lineage of 'generative' literature that emerges from the intersection of Stein's grammar experiments and Strachey's mathematisation of literature. Queneau's text realises the vast number of sonnets from the title through ten printed sonnets, sliced into lines and attached along the left margin. The lines within each group 'work' in combination with any other – they follow the rhyme scheme of a sonnet and result in a grammatically correct whole. Lines cannot move from their horizontal position on the page, and only one of a given line can be shown at any time (for example, line 2 from sonnet 1 cannot be combined with line 2 of sonnet 2). Regardless of this limitation, the potential meanings of the poem multiply massively in excess of what is readable in any one lifetime.

The contemporary versioning of this kind of impossibly large potential from a relatively small number of variables is the basis for many works of electronic literature. Such works often use basic HTML or JavaScript and consist of a digital text whose components change depending on a given set of variables: the online iterations often change as we are looking at them. Some of these works, such as J. R. Carpenter's *Etheric Ocean* (2016) and *Notes on the Voyage of Owl and Girl* (2014), have also been made available as printed and performance versions. In Carpenter's print versions of born-digital poems, the flow forward of the text stops at a given moment, and several iterations are shown as a list:

> According to my ['calculations', 'library books', 'test results'], the girl informed the owl, it's ['six', 'seventeen', 'twenty-seven'] ['leagues', 'knots', 'nights', 'nautical miles'] ['due north', 'north', 'northeast'] of here. Her ['mother', 'great-aunt', 'grandmother'] had been among the most revered of ['authors', 'experts', 'philosophers'] on this topic. But the girl had her own ['life to live', 'line of inquiry', 'ideas', 'theories'] (Carpenter 2014)

Perhaps this gesture invites the reader to select from the options displayed, but equally, we can read it as a kind of stutter, hovering and flickering at a single moment in a grammar, evoking odd syntactical repetitions. Carpenter's published versions of these works are post-digital in that their repetitive syntax is drawn from executable code conventions, making these conventions strange by rendering them in print and inviting us (rather than machines) to execute them. As you select your version of this poem, you become the protocol by which its meaning is made and so become aware of the arbitrariness that underlies the computer's seeming generative magic. Coding mark-up is a neat, subtly critical tool in this sense, and Carpenter's readings of these works correspond with the kinds of pressure displayed in Scourti's performances. The fact that limited databases of text can be called on in ways that can be said to be 'generative', i.e. making new, is due to the large number of ways they can be combined, which produces a sense of scale in which each combination is unique. However, this method of automating 'scale' is an analogue era invention and quite different from the algorithms that draw on mutable corpora.

Predictive Text

The personalised dictionary that underpins predictive text technology is an example point at which the English language, though still the 'language of interoperability' (Bergvall in Thurston 2011, 45), is being defused by the technical situation. The cultural colonialism of the

English language presiding over print and broadcast media has been loosened by a media situation in which the language is arbitrated across multiple globalised platforms iterated by computers.

Using the way that different corpus sets are networked in 'National Language: Sixteen Translations From English Into English', the poet Ross Sutherland (2011) feeds famous English poems into translation software, translating them into various languages before returning them to English and back again. Each translation causes 'the poem to mutate in new unexpected directions' after travelling across the global lexica. Sometimes the language glitches that result resemble Murata's datamoshed videos, especially in cases where semantic excess blooms from relatively small prompts. For example, Ezra Pound's canonical two-line poem 'In Station of the Metro', 'The apparition of these faces in the crowd:/Petals on a wet, black bough', becomes a sixteen-line surrealist verse, each line of which contains a ghostly, diffuse trace of the original, as in these excerpts:

> My internal multiplicity breaks
> inside this illusion of a face,
> [...]
> in the midst of a hallucination
> of wood and maple, it maintains its variety–
> [...]
> I know I am approaching a gap in the Earth,
> here in this capital of dangerous colours.
> (Sutherland 2011)

As with datamoshing, this glitch poetry method offers an acutely limited amount of control and gives a voice to a previously unseen set of technical relations impressing themselves on what English is. As Sutherland observes, learning to operate the translators is primarily a process of anticipating the tensions between concision and accuracy embedded in the computational space at the intersection of different languages relative to their English language original. The 'poetry happens' in the correspondences between English and the various languages that are coded into Babelfish's translate programme.

As Scourti's work astutely draws out, another of the connective strands in 'natural language processing' is the voice. The artist Anna Barham works in this space of voice and computer comprehension, pushing the voice into the computer system and glitching it. In her group reading exercises, she exploits the slippages that occur when speech-to-text software is presented with different accents in quick succession. Barham amplifies the errors that occur when software misrecognises the voice by having her participants reread the resulting textual errors back into the software, producing an additive feedback cycle in which it amplifies its misunderstandings, causing assonant-like strings of error. Its errors further evolve the source text from its original into a wholly new vocabulary. Barham exhibits the resulting texts as wall-prints (fig. 8) that juxtapose the source text with its successive glitch iterations, inviting us to read down through the slippages of the human

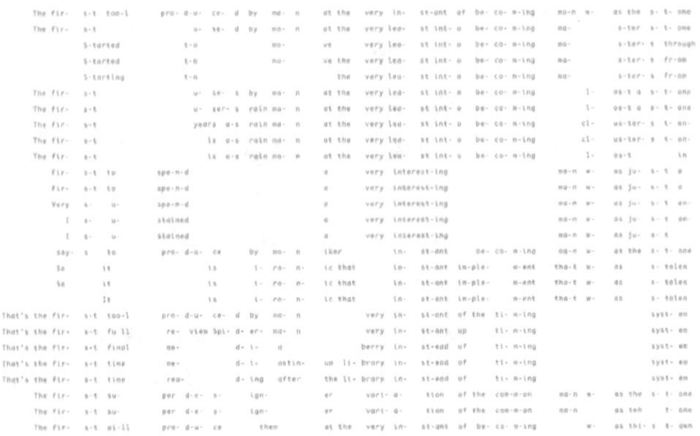

Fig. 8. Anna Barham, Knives, print on blueback paper pasted to wall, 4x1.8 m, 2017. Courtesy of the artist.

voice understood by a machine. In *Knives* (2017), the various stages of Barham's process are laid out, so the mistakes made by the voice-to-text software can be read down the columns: 'at the very instant of becoming' becomes 'at the very least into becoming' and then 'a very interesting' and 'iker instant becoming' and the library instead of timing', and the gaps left by the process produce small islands of homophonic relation.

The experience of reading the maps of homophones and gaps emerging from the crafted and automated processes Barham uses is affectively disorienting. The logics with which computers connect and infer from human input flicker at the limit of what we can empathise and comprehend. In the case of Scourti's work the computer's 'language' is established by combining a limited stock of phrases and word-combinations established by the artist. Nevertheless, it is the way the machine uses these combinations to make something that appears to be 'thought out' but is thought wrongly that is discomforting.

The glitches in Scourti's voice as she speaks the computer language give texture to a particular language discomfort. By embodying these errors performatively, Scourti is pointing towards the inherent misfit in our relationship with computers as we flip from being the users of technology to being used by it. Her voice evokes a distance between human ingenuity and struggle, and the machine's insistence on a kind of forward movement through its algorithmic steps. Works of this nature are inherently temporal, cataloguing a moment when we *can* tell what is human-written from what is not by decerning something in its texture. However, our uncertainty evokes an era, immanent certainly, where such textures will be even more fine-grained, disappearing into the high gloss synthetic world, when it will seem not to matter.

The flickering oscillation of glitch poetics suggests we are at a boundary moment in language evolution. That the boundary language which results from the artistic and critical experiments of Scourti, Sutherland and Barham has an expressly, recognisably contemporary texture can be understood through the lens of what Braidotti and Hlavajava call 'the posthuman predicament' (2018, 1), and can be further explored in its contemporary context through comparison with another work by Bergvall.

The Posthuman Predicament

In a talk titled 'The Contested Posthumanities' in Liverpool during the early stages of gathering *The Posthuman Glossary,* Braidotti (2016) observed that 'language is cracking and compressing under the pressure of the Anthropocene'. This comment fuses the social conditions for contemporary language to the ecological conditions of a new geological age and suggests a transversal movement of crisis, as it runs through rocks into the written word. The current condition requires neologisms as makeshift, temporally specific responses to new linkages of systems exemplified by the Anthropocene. Like the Anthropocene's physical hybrids, these words most often take the form of recombinations, portmanteau that articulate new overlaps of meanings, cultures and materials. *The Posthuman Glossary* is an archive of such linguistic overlaps: 'What could terms such as "altergorithm", "rewilding", "negentropy" and "technoanimalism" possibly have in common? ... [T]hey are all neologisms that attempt to come to terms with the complexities of the posthuman predicament' (Braidotti and Hlavajava 2018, 6). It is not just scholarship that has had to find a new language for current conditions. Under the pressure of an increasingly hybridised relation to technology that demands extreme physical and cognitive adaptations to innovation, the broader linguistic environment is changing rapidly too. Our collective consciousness is increasingly globalised and subjected to the unpredictable proximities of an unknowably complex media climate.

Linguistic anomalies enter the fault-lines opened in the English language as it traces newly combined events, subcultures, networks and crowd usages.

To retain its position at the centre of the global communicative infrastructures, English has had to branch outside of the established monoliths of language production and oversight, such as printed dictionaries, and blend itself into the network. Lexical corpora stored on individuals' phones and in cloud computing 'vaults' act as archives of the bifurcation of 'authorised' language. Words such as *Brangelina, bae, bigly,* and *Brexit* are no sooner uttered than they are entered into a massively distributed set of personal and public dictionaries, and weighted for their likelihood in relation to a digital profile of the user held in cloud storage. The result is a permanently unsettled lexical environment in which phones, voices, slangs, computers, journalists, trendsetters, local knowledges and online platforms such as Urban Dictionary, Wiktionary, Google Mail and the Evernote app that Scourti uses mix and combine prediction with diction, in a process that is for the most part separated from the print-dominated cultures and inconsequently tiny circulations of poetry.

Of course, there has always been a lively set of aberrant vocabularies, often tied to distinct regional or subcultural groupings as vernaculars, dialects and slangs,[20] but the current combination of technological means and political fragmentation has led to an increasing marginalisation of lexical authorities. New, fluid lexical records amplify their own 'errors' in ways that recall earlier, oral cultures. The collective language glitches and blossoms across the network indexing it to similar error amplification and language evolutions from history.

Meddle English

Bergvall's work *Meddle English* suggests that the Anthropocene's new lexical environment marks the end of a period of linguistic stability that only began with the invention of the printing press in the fourteenth century. In the essay which opens *Meddle English* (2011, 5), consisting of 'three points: the middle, the meddle, the midden', Bergvall states that the 'midden' is the space where the old and outmoded – bones, letterforms, vowel sounds, and machinery – interrelate: 'letters sounds words are discarded from a language during accidental breaks. Or dispensed with, like outmoded cooking utensils. Or pulled out like teeth. Entire jawlines of these' (6). Bergvall describes the midden as a kind of compost, a wastage of forgotten machines, geologies and human habits, that constitutes the conditions for contemporary language. The poems in *Meddle English* are an act of media archaeology that 'cuts into' modern English's 'totemic stacks', exposing in the strata of their various stages these suppressed and forgotten odds and ends.

> To meddle with English ... is a process of social and mental excavation explored to a point of extremity. One that reaches for the irritated, excitable uncertainties of our embodied spoken

> lives by working with, taking apart, seeing through the imposed complicities of linguistic networks and cultural scaffolds (Bergvall 2011, 18).

The reinvocation of qualities of language from the pre-printing press era in this book, Bergvall suggests, is a return to 'language in the making' (Thurston 2012, 82): a return that excavates contemporary language 'to a point of extremity', where its glitching, malfunctioning mannerisms are reimagined as new vernacular possibilities.

In *Noping*, the 2013 online animated text and vocal work that marks the 'beginning of a descent into the building stacks of language' for Bergvall, the artist isolates the history of the Nordic *thorn* glyph,Þ, as a point of reference. The direct result of the standardisation of type to suit printing press mechanics, the *thorn* was made obsolete in favour of an Anglophone alphabet 'th', and therefore disappeared from usage at this time, along with the Celtic 'eth', ð. Bergvall describes her interest in the *thorn* as 'an index of what remains for me an unreadable, largely unpronounceable historic language' (Bergvall, 2013).

In the *Noping* poem, Bergvall performs and reinscribes the missing, obsolete glyph (which resembles a combination of the modern 'b' and 'p') by sounding 'Þ' in place of each instance of 'th' in an original poem: so 'no*th*ing' becomes 'no-*p*ing'. Through this corruption of the technical standards that derive the spoken from the written, the poem performs 'an unexpected tripping into English-language history. A poem in which *noping* is where *nothing* was'.

> It's a fine day · you step on to the top soil of your
> strata · you trip over someþing nearly makes
> you fall over ·
>
> (Bergvall 2013)

This gesture of the glitch here, a single logic error that progressively malforms and corrupts Bergvall's language, is also a semantic device: showing-telling what it is to trip, to be stopped in your tracks and have your attention drawn to 'some-*þ*ing'. With a characteristic conceptual neatness, the letter *sticks into,* cuts, irritates the text. The contingent relation of letterforms to tongue gestures is performed as a connective fabric with Bergvall's Nordic roots, affirming a 'personal matter' to the enunciation, one which speaks directly to the increasingly diverse and personal instances of the language-corpus that underpin predictive text. The letter, once extinct, is conspicuously present in Bergvall's reading.

The 'middling' of English – disrupting and recentring modern English with citations of its middle-age tendencies – has a particular contemporary potency that concerns predictive text and personal dictionaries. The popularity and originality of Chaucer's poetry in the fourteenth-century, poetry which itself fed willingly on medieval French and Italian languages, influenced the standardisation of English during this period (Giancarlo 2009). This effect was stratified into the mainstream language by the spread of the printing press. Bergvall's poems in *Middling English* use a macaronic combination of English language from different times to undo the work of technologically and poetically driven standardisation. Bergvall's contemporary glitch poetics draw from history in their deployment of an irregular and inconsistent 'untimely' lexicon.

At times in *Meddle English* Bergvall performs the instability of Middle English's variant spellings as a form of repetition. Deploying several spellings for the same word in the same phrase allows Bergvall to condense the lexical irregularities of Middle English onto single lines. For example: 'A new ideology of yvele evell evyl evil manaces society' (32), and 'I walk and I walke, I fish and I fisshe' (33). Though Middle English spellings are notoriously volatile, the words as we currently pronounce them are audibly similar to their modern equivalents. We say 'fish' and 'fisshe' the same, for example. As a result, and contrasting usefully with the effortfully bodily errors of 'About Face', our reading of Bergvall's repetitions in the extracts above is characterised by an effortful silence: we see the words as different, but these differences become spectral as we voice them. These poems move forward through difference, but our relation to them requires an inefficient, ghostly hesitancy, destabilising the fluency of modern English, the 'language of interoperability', with a much more contingent and an uncannily sensuous lightness. Reading these poems, I suggest, our voices glitch into the past of our pre-colonial English language, back to a history that, as we have observed, inscribes its instabilities into the present as 'new media'.

Conclusion

The combination of technological evolutions and ruptures, and postcolonial perspectives in *Meddle English* is emblematic of the possibilities that Braidotti identifies in the posthumanist trajectory. As Scourti emphasises with regard to her work, 'Identity emerges as much from the networks and infrastructures that we inhabit and are entangled within, as it does from any sense of a coherent interior essence ... [based in] older conceptions of self' (Scourti 2015). Our encounters with the works in this chapter show that our sense of what language can convey develops through error.

Reading across texts and technologies in the way I have done here draws attention to the unique proximity of media and biological systems in contemporary language: a glitchfrastructure composed of acts of reading, writing and the related maintenance or evolution of word- and letter-meanings. The overlaps of media and biology in language history are replicated in the overlaps between the practices of innovative language and glitch artists. Both sets of practitioners articulate the aesthetic and critical benefits of 'meddlings' or 'tactics' that emphasise the sensory response to glitch events. They also both frequently dive into histories of media, or historicise current media conditions, to gesture towards alternative ways of organising body-machine relations, identifying contradictions in the way things are.

I have appropriated Lauren Berlant's term glitchfrastructure to imply that the 'living mediation' produced in the moment of glitch can itself constitute a new model of interaction. To cope with a glitch requires unconventional activity in devices and people alike, and the potentials of this (as we read a 'difficult' text, for example, or as a machine is forced to understand multiple voices with different accents) are central to glitch poetics, rather than being a side effect of their difficulty. It is in the specific way of adapting to temporary glitches – what makes glitches temporary at all – that one system expresses its limits and communicates these extents to another. In the work of Scourti and Bergvall this process of adaptation acts as a connective tissue between readers and writers. In turn, this opens onto the implication that the ambient presence of media technologies can express itself as error in the literary sphere, which is the subject of my next chapter.

Chapter 2

Lyric-Code Glitch

The written word of the post-digital age is infected, perhaps compromised, perhaps augmented, by the temporalities and structures of computational code. Indeed, the term 'code' has a history that predates its current associations with computers. As suggested in the introduction to this book, pre-digital uses of code are implicit in the 'codified' rhetoric of poetry and kabbalistic literature, which obscure and reveal their meanings only under certain conditions, like magic spells. Now that code's dominant meaning refers to computer-readable language, language itself is subject to a substantial, if mostly hidden, non-human agency. Shintaro Miyazaki uses the neologism 'algorhythmics' to describe how the built-in time functions and executability of coded algorithms form a 'machinic reality': 'An algorhythm is the result of an inter-play, orchestration and synthesis of abstract algorithmic and calculable organisational concepts, with real-world rhythmic signals, which have measurable physical properties' (Miyazaki 2012)'. Wolfgang Ernst suggests that coded phenomena are 'micro-archival' in nature, operating at temporal scales below the threshold of human experience. The inherent mutability of what is archived when recalled through these processes results in an 'irritated present' for us: a sense of unreality or instability that we embody as psychological effects (Ernst 2017, 1). This chapter concerns itself with two poets who push the psychological presence of code as executable and micro-archival language to the surface of their poems.

Glitch poetics serves as a digital-age metaphor for a phenomenon that preceded the digital – the verbal corruption – which now strangely reveals something of a pervasive digital quality. N. Katherine Hayles uses this figure in her writing, noting that it hovers 'between a proposition and an analogy': 'Code is the unconscious of language… just as the unconscious surfaces through significant puns, slips, and metonymic splices, so the underlying code surfaces at those moments when [a word processing] program makes decisions we have not consciously initiated' (Hayles 2006). Hayles refers to the auto-correct function on her word processor, which 'appears' only when she makes a type-written mistake. She relates this to the notion of the 'Freudian slip', or *parapraxis*, used to name the moment a trace of the unconscious appears in the mistaken but prescient utterance. The implication here is that glitches in language technics operate, like Freudian parapraxes, to show beneath what is immediately apparent, giving a glimpse into how the complex systems that relate us to machines – and to each other – are structured. Freud describes the revealing linguistic slip as parapraxis (literally *para* – beside/beyond – and *praxis* – to act) because it is a moment in which what is beyond apprehension, the uncommunicable, or unthinkable, can be 'acted out' through a breakdown in conscious action (Freud 1995 [1901], 53-67). Parapraxis happens both in verbal slips and in dreams. Indeed, evoking the connection between error, weirdness and unknowable complexity, dreaming is frequently used as a figure for the kinds of processes happening beneath the surface of advanced software. For example, Google's Deep Dream is a reverse-engineered software that can be applied to existing images (fig. 9a & b). It reveals how complex 'neural network' programmes process information, seeking patterns, and thus producing a view on the sub-temporal, virtual world of processing that would be unavailable by looking at the input, script and output (Temperton 2015).

As we have seen in the work of Erica Scourti, performative interactions with writing technologies offer a mode for pushing the formerly intangible tendencies of their data-processing to the surface and highlighting their politics. In what follows, I suggest that a poetics of error can also reveal something about our proximity to, and absorption of, code whose tendencies we have sublimated.

I explore the subliminal effects of computer code by reading how it is rendered – or 'negatively figured' – by the glitch poetics of contemporary lyrics. The examples I use in this chapter are Ben Lerner's *Mean Free Path* (2010) and Keston Sutherland's *The Odes to TL61P* (2013), both of

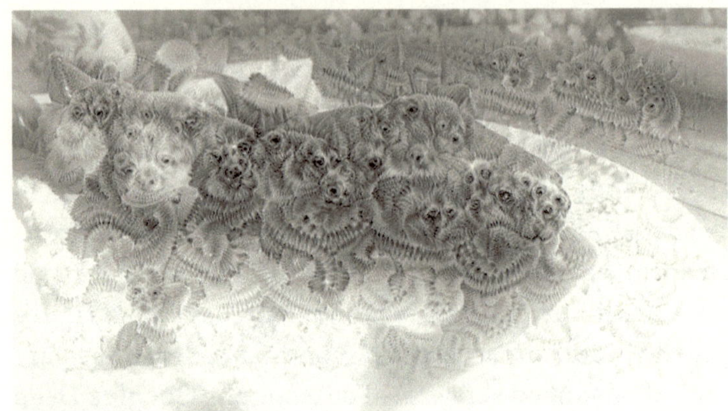

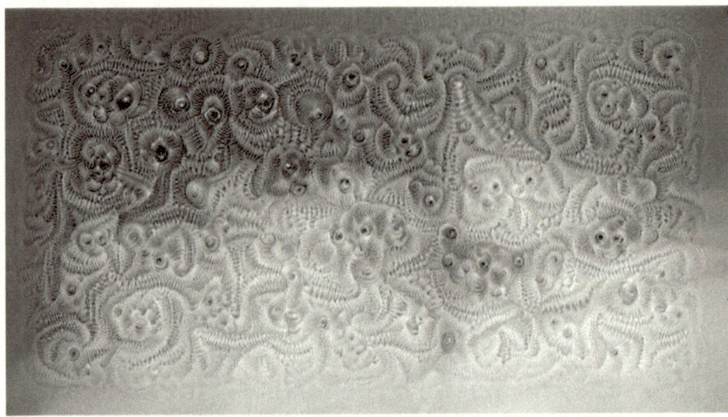

Figs. 9a and 9b. Images from the preface to this book, run through RunwayML's instantiation of the Google Deep Dream API (2021).

which have garnered considerable acclaim and imitation[21] on both sides of the Atlantic, capturing in different ways new methods by which the lyric can respond to the contemporary moment. In these books, Lerner and Sutherland provide clear indications of a relatively rare post-digital mode for contemporary poetry: theirs is literature that emphasises the instabilities and problems of digital age communication, even as it admits to the absolute saturation of contemporary experience in digital processes and therefore the impossibility of writing (and reading) outside of them. To crystalise this point, I will read these works alongside close readings of digital technologies and digital art.

Reading into glitches across media cultures and literary forms gives an essential update on the depth of the entanglements of politics, culture and technology that Walter Benjamin and Theodor Adorno concerned themselves with during the opening phases of commercial and technological modernity. The post-digital poetry of Lerner and Sutherland is a contemporary form of what Benjamin and Adorno called 'immanent critique': writing from within the contradictions and incompatibilities of current societal conditions, particularly those that offer significant potential for emancipation from capitalist alienation (Antonio 1981, 330). Written through the logic of immanent critique, the presence and pervasiveness of computer code forces the heightened, personalised language of lyric poetry into a new awareness of its role as storing and executing a poet's expressive intent. Lerner and Sutherland make their poems glitch at the boundaries between the 'actual' and the 'virtual', 'truth' and 'wrongness', 'word' and 'action'; suggesting – rightly, I think – that in a world where code-driven systems have proliferated to the extent that they overwhelm social and political influence over the public sphere, the context for poetry has been radically altered. The lyric's historical continuity from earlier eras of poetic radicalism to now, and its particular position as a heightened form of self-expression at the interface with politics, make it an ideal form through which to observe how language has changed; specifically, that what we consider errors in language might be textural dashes of realism shaped by contemporaneous technical factors.

Lerner and Sutherland diagnose the ways contemporary language internalises the digital condition differently from one another, in part because of their respective theoretical grounding in Benjaminian and Adornian thought. Lerner's work can appear reticent, as though coy about its relationship to an ethically unsound linguistic environment. His work operates as a kind of static, a high-frequency motion in which unforeseen constellations of meaning can occur. Sutherland's operates more iconoclastically, as though he is attempting to prove the reader wrong, to break (or re-programme) our relationship to the language we take for granted, with the work jerking and shuddering. In both books, the conventional readability of language as carrying meaning and information is exchanged in return for a demanding encounter with the systems behind it. In *Mean Free Path* and *The Odes to TL61P*, we encounter the compromises the language of the lyric faces today at the threshold between what is readable and what is unreadable in them. Glitches in lyric poetry emphasise the pervasiveness of digital forms and put the digital rhetoric of 'virtuality', 'immateriality' and 'efficiency' in tension with topics that are more traditionally associated with the lyric, such as self-realisation, feelings and the life and death of human subjects (Jackson and Prins 2014, 8). The language that results suggests a problematic, even traumatic situation for individuals seeking to express themselves today, using a language whose circulation they only partially control or understand.

Lerner specifically suggests that his engagement with today's ambient code environment aims to clarify what today's language situation is. In an interview he says, 'we all know we can't do anything that isn't shot through with capital, but we also want to figure the outside – you can make works that can negatively figure what they can't actualise' (in Clune 2016). Sutherland also considers the poem to be involved in capitalism's saturation of social relations. He sees capital in its essentially bureaucratic forms in certain aspects of the digital, which his poetry both apes and looks to decouple from codes for living. In different ways, the glitch-ontology of Sutherland's and Lerner's lyrics as they flicker between critique and replication of the digital language situation offer an after-image of what they *cannot* say within their poems, and of what poetry *cannot* do with what it says.

This emphasis on the limits of what can be said and done sets the stage for different kinds of personal confession to blend into political declaration in their work. As Sutherland suggests in an interview in the *White Review*:

> It is crucial to my conception of the present limits of poetic eloquence that there really is a significant material difference between writing poetry and being a politically effective agent in the world. … That for me is a problem, but it is also a fact that can be endlessly explored and reflected on from an infinite variety of angles. I try to do that with The Odes, to explore the limits not only of agency but of inertia and of impotence. (in Ferris 2013)

Lyric Poetry and Immanent Critique

For Benjamin and Adorno, the lyric of modernity was pregnant with the twin possibilities of being an expression of the *Zeitgeist* – a 'beacon of social progress' – and a 'folk' expression of the common citizenry or proletariat (Jackson and Prins 2014, 320). However, even in the late nineteenth century, this possibility expressed itself only as a negation: 'social progress' meant that the emerging modern reader had been alienated from culture by the reification of their labour, and that their alienation from the social inheritance of the lyric was a synecdoche for their alienation from the society as a whole. As Benjamin states directly in the opening of *Baudelaire's Paris*: 'Baudelaire envisaged readers to whom the reading of lyric poetry would present difficulties' (Benjamin 2003, 313). The difficulty of reconciling lyric poetry with the social context of a readership is intensified in the work of Lerner and Sutherland through the motif and methods of corrupted language. Both poets address their readers directly in their books, suggesting that the readers' own difficulty running and reading the poems is their point. Sutherland states at the beginning of *TL61P*:

> And the situation is like that in certain games, in which all places on the board are supposed to be filled in accordance with certain rules, where at the end, blocked by certain spaces, you will be forced to leave more places empty than you could have or wanted to, unless you used some trick. There is, however, a certain procedure through which one can most easily fill the board.
>
> Wake up my fellow citizens and middle class and go look into the mirror. (Sutherland 2013, 3)

It is evident in this passage at the beginning of the poem that Sutherland's work is an immanent critique of the 'game' of digital capitalism, albeit one that a poem is likely to lose. Lerner, in a strikingly candid moment in *Mean Free Path,* also addresses his readers: 'My numb / Rebarbative people', he commands us, 'put down your Glocks / And your Big Gulps' (Lerner 2010, 32).[22] Contrasting Sutherland's almost tragically emphatic 'wake-up my fellow citizens', Lerner's 'my numb rebarbative people' ironically satirises the idea that poetry can command anything, especially in a world of violently amplified voices of commercial, broadcast and celebrity cultures. Lerner's admission that a proletariat readership is unlikely to be reached, let alone be awakened (perhaps 'woke'?) from social conditions by his work, directly reflects the influence of melancholic

Benjaminian thinking on the poet. In the world of *Mean Free Path,* multiple readers, authors and meanings are possible for a language that mutates and reiterates itself, but the consequence of these is muted by the economies of scale in today's affectively dense media environments. The distribution networks, intensities and volumes of the internet swamp the potential of the small, poorly read, inconsequential poem. Lerner puts this notion into operation by making his verse like a sequence of encoded clues seeking an encryption key, pulling itself apart and piecing itself back together in innumerable, arbitrary ways.

Lerner 'performs' the notion of a digital age poem as an arbitrary recombination of words by repeating phrases through his poems, each time in a slightly mutated form. For example, this typical sequence found in the early pages of the book features a set of recurring phrases, recombined until their final startling iteration: 'I'm writing this one as a woman / Comfortable with failure' (9); 'Reference is a woman / Comfortable with failure' (11); 'I'm writing this one / With my non-dominant hand in the crawlspace' (14); 'I'm writing this one / As a woman comfortable with leading / A prisoner on a leash' (15). As illustrated in the last of this sequence of excerpts, the tension in these poems is that even arbitrary reconfiguration throws up the potential for 'shocks' to happen in the text. The last phrase cites images of abusive practices in the Abu Ghraib US military prison in Baghdad exposed by a 2003 data leak; reading it, we are forced to review our position on the poem's voice. The glimpses of reality we were given by the previous iterations – the gender play of 'I'm writing this one as a woman', the notion of ease in 'comfortable with failure' – were not what we thought they were. This final 'woman comfortable' rearticulates each of the previous iterations as broken, partial attempts to speak in the language of someone depicted in the act of intolerable cruelty. Though we should note that, in the non-linear world of *Mean Free Path,* nothing in particular suggests this 'final' reading should predominate over the others.

The conception of the poem as the site of atemporal meetings, in which poetic truth can be rendered only through collisions and shocks emanating from encounters with the poem, the poem's worlds, and the poem's encounter with itself, is a technique that Lerner inherits from Benjamin and adapts for a digital context by echoing Benjamin's term, the 'dialectical image' (Benjamin 2003, 45). Benjamin's formulation must be considered as deeply entwined with the dominant image-making medium of his time, and so Lerner's version of dialectical images must be thought through the conditions of our own image-making methods.

Benjamin's Baudelaire

For Benjamin, Baudelaire is the first modern poet because he is the first to open his work to the emerging commodity-capitalist metropolis, where 'the exposure to shock has become the norm' (Benjamin 2003, 318). Of the lines 'And, minute by minute, Time engulfs me, / The way an immense snowfall engulfs a body grown stiff' in Baudelaire's 1857 collection *Les Fleur de Mals*, Benjamin says, 'The hidden constellation – in which the profound beauty of that stanza becomes thoroughly transparent – is no doubt a phantom crowd: the words, the fragments, the beginnings of lines, from which the poet, in the deserted streets, wrests poetic booty' (Benjamin 2003, 323). The shock of Baudelaire's modernity is embodied in the figure of the crowd, which is 'nowhere named' in Baudelaire's poems, but is 'imprinted on his creativity as a hidden figure' (321-3). Baudelaire's crowd surveying and buying commodities is the reified human environment administered by commodity capitalism, which dissolves the lyric subject's unique voice, but from which, nevertheless, a unique poetic vision is rendered.

There are notable resonances between the Baudelaire of Benjamin, particularly the 'hidden constellation' of the crowd, and the similarly transparent but disordering presence of the digital protocol in Lerner's poetry. In the same way that an understanding of Lerner's poetry is inseparable from today's informatic commercial and media-sphere, the crowd-metropolis of early modernity produces the distinctive texture and affect in Baudelaire's. Despite the fact they are not explicitly named, the internet and the crowd form veils through which we experience Lerner and Baudelaire's poems. Vitally, Benjamin is keen that we understand Baudelaire through the contemporaneous technical conditions of the emergent metropolis: in particular, how his 'poetic images' echo the predominant method for representing the world of its day, the daguerreotype photograph (fig. 10). In the opening sections of his work on Baudelaire, Benjamin portrays the poet using terminology from the emergent field of photography:

An image to characterise Baudelaire's way of looking at the world. Let us compare time to a photographer – earthly time to a photographer who photographs the essence of things. But because of the nature of earthly time and its apparatus, the photographer manages only to register the negative of that essence on his photographic plates. No one can read these plates; no one can deduct from the negative, on which time records the objects, the true essence of things as they really are. Moreover, the elixir that might act as a developing agent is unknown. And there is Baudelaire: he doesn't possess the vital fluid either – the fluid in which these plates would have to be immersed so as to obtain the true picture. But he, he alone, is able to read the plates, thanks to infinite mental efforts. He alone is able to extract from the negatives of essence a presentiment of its real picture. And from this presentiment speaks the negative of essence in all his poems. (Benjamin 2006, 27)

The ability to perceive how time is rendered by the city is the poet's unique gift, and through this, he sees the city emerging.

Clearly, the notion of the 'elixir' is drawn from the then-recent invention of the chemical production of images. Indeed, much of Benjamin's philosophy evokes the ghostly quality of the particular errors in the analogue era of reproduction. As seen in this example (fig.

10), an 1840 rendering of a Paris street by the technique's inventor Louis Daguerre, the daguerreotype process resulted in the strong presence of chemical marks around the edges of the image, with parts of the image dissolving into whiteness. In his photo, buildings appear to rise through a cloud of chemicals, analogous to the dust raised by a crowd or the noise of people's voices and clothes as they bustle through the street. The only human figure to be seen in the image below appears as a 'phantom' vanishing into his own movement, while the sky and shadows between buildings contain evocative and patternless clusters of line and fragment, perhaps people who are vanishing into the past. In the manner of Google Deep Dream, we can also see the pattern of an eye forming in the bottom right, under the eaves of the house. But what is most striking about this image is the absence of the crowd: but this is an illusion brought about by the image-making process, which requires things to stay still for ten minutes or more in order to be rendered on the photo plate.

The daguerreotype process produced error effects that informed Benjamin's notion of the crowd as an absent force in Baudelaire's poetry. To apply an analogous notion the visual image to Lerner's image-making, we should consider how storage and recall functions in the image flows of the digital age. Rather than a developing fluid, the elixir of the contemporary moment is a code, or rather coding-decoding mechanisms called 'codecs', and their effects can also be seen as forms of temporality in its error artefacts.

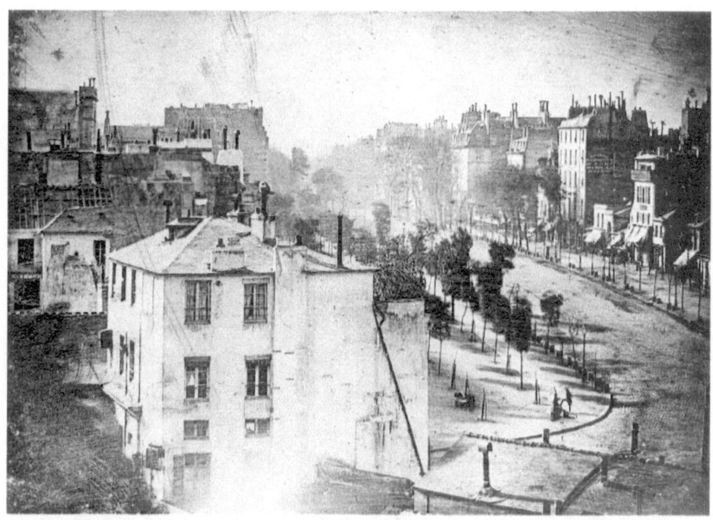

Fig. 10. Louis Daguerre, Boulevard du Temple, 1838.
Public Domain.

The media archaeologist Wolfgang Ernst describes as an 'ecstatic temporality' (Ernst 2017, 23) the media condition by which various layers and scales of time flow across and through digital images and sound as they are produced by codecs. Ernst observes that all media in the digital is 'micro-archival', and therefore its record of the past is inseparable from the material contingencies of the present. The faces and voices of digital media are simultaneously of the past – arriving from the storage data they have been packed into for transmission – and are totally contingent on present-moment interfaces, themselves flowing and flickering at different speeds: from LCD composition to algorithmic calculation, to the binary flickering of a silicon chip. We encounter a frozen form of this 'irritation of

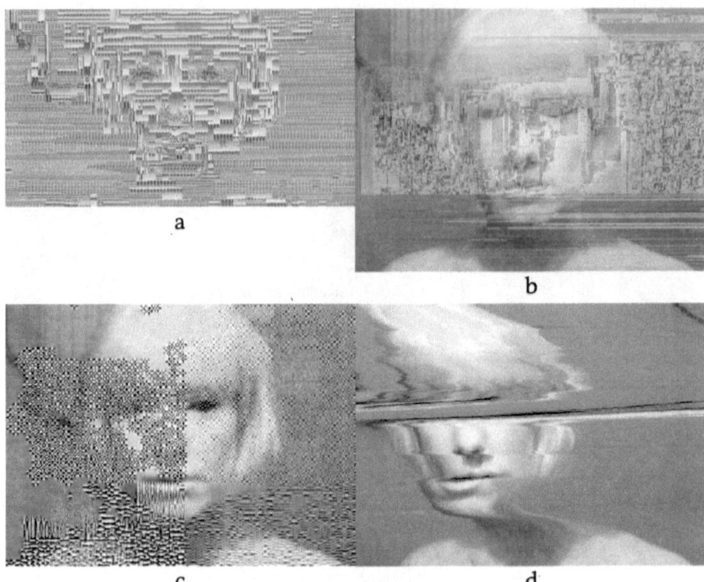

Figs 11a-d. Screenshots from Rosa Menkman's A Vernacular of File Formats, 2010. Used with permission. A Vernacular of File Formats takes the form of a series of distorted, warped, striated and pixilated images, with information on how Menkman altered the data structure of the image file or the interface that showed it. Fig. 11a was produced by using the USPEC file format, 'the weirdest file format around' according to the Rhizome website. Fig. 11b was produced by bending the PNG codec. Fig. 11c was produced by bending the JPG2000 codec. Fig. 11d produced by bending the BMP codec.

the present' as a texture in the glitch's visual or audible artefacts.

In *A Vernacular of File Formats* (2010b) (figs. 11a-d), Menkman illustrates the diversity of micro-archival processes involved in storing and displaying digital images. By interfering with – or 'bending' – the code protocols that decode the image data, Menkman causes them to reveal the temporal dialectics of source code and surface appearance in image display. The 'irritation of the present' of digital media usually happens below the threshold of human perception, but we see it here in operation.

The subliminal temporality of codec operations suggests for Ernst a psychic restructuring of contemporary experience. 'Human physiology and neuronal cognition are affected by such signal processing and signal transmitting technologies. In subliminal perception, there are tempo-real traumata which do not stem from individual or social interaction but are induced by the media shock of technological timings itself' (Ernst 2017, 12). The forms of ultra-speed transmission, measuring, and processing taking place within the switches and diodes and sub-routines of digital media affect human bodies and thinking in ways that constitute a traumatic environment, and it is this environment that Lerner writes from.

Mean Free Path

In *Mean Free Path* (published in the same year as Menkman's glitched images), the temporal irritation of digital culture is reflected in the notion of mutable poetic images and in the paradoxical conflation of contact and loss. As Lerner – or the narrator in the poems – says: 'A live tradition broadcast with a little delay / Takes the place of experience' (Lerner 2010, 14). Like the codes that produce Menkman's digital images, *Mean Free Path* contains the rapid temporalities of media in a static form, as error. We perceive the digital's atmosphere through the odd static flows that populate the text as collision, repetition and misplacement, like the pixels in Menkman's images.

The idea of still, shifted time also works as a motif in the poems. Neither the surface effect nor the motion of the rain is allowed to predominate in the passage below; instead, we encounter a glitching threshold between 'rain' as a virtual category and its surface appearance on the window – or rather, on the city of Denver – as a corruption.

> I planned a work that could describe itself
> Into existence, then back out again
> Until description yielded to experience
> ...
> Dusk. Look out of the window. Those small
> Rain. In a holding pattern over Denver
> Collisions clear a path from ground to cloud.
> (Lerner 2010, 49)

Such self-reflexive moments serve as allegories of the (de)composition of the poem as a whole and connect Lerner's process to the codified form of the contemporary image. The poem's corrupted surface does 'describe itself/ into existence / and then back out again'. If an image can bring itself into existence, it can also dissolve. As a line depicts this tension in a telephone conversation that embodies the innate glitchiness of contemporary relations: 'you're / Breaking up. No, down' (Lerner 2010, 17).

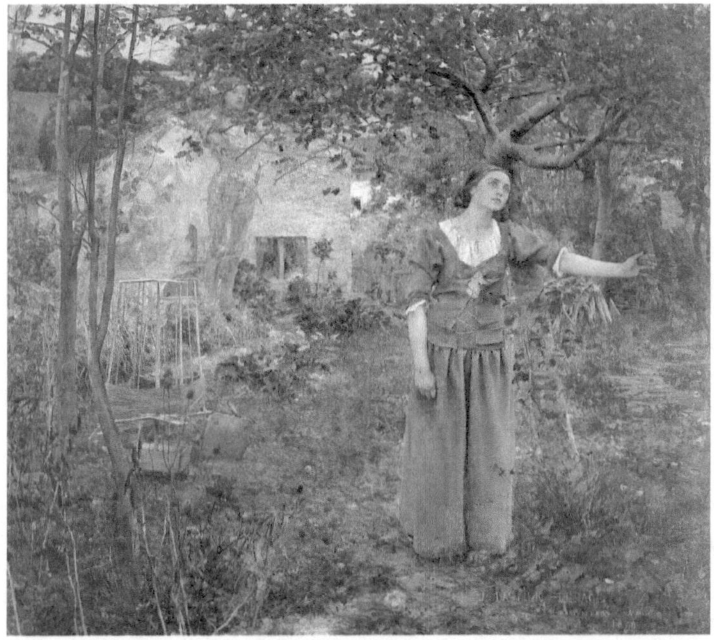

Fig. 12. Jules Bastien-Lepage, Joan of Arc, 1879. Public Domain.

In the first pages of his 2015 novel *10:04*, Lerner invokes the digital glitch to describe a part of the French artist Jules Bastien-Lepage's 1879 painting *Joan of Arc* (fig. 12), clearly influenced by the chemical distortions of the daguerreotype in the nineteenth century, in which the subject's hand is not completely distinguished from the background: 'It's as if the tension between the metaphysical and physical worlds, between two orders of temporality, produces a glitch in the pictorial matrix; the background swallows her fingers' (Lerner 2015, 10).

As Lerner's character in the novel observes, evoking Ernst's diagnosis of the digital condition in which times flow into the image in an ecstatic, atemporal fashion, the confusion of layers in the image might be a formal lack in which the hand is lost, but it also gestures towards a temporal excess: 'It's a presence that eats her hand ... the presence of the future' (10). This moment is a good guide to the kinds of disturbed imagery we find in the *Mean Free Path* poems.

For Lerner, this painting operates as a figure for the poem as an act of remembering that is radically dependent on its presentness and even futurity: as we have observed, *Mean Free Path's* poetic images are often meeting places for formal and semantic excess that rely on past and present occurrences of an image or phrase. Just as Lerner's character notes that the visual record of the painter's 'failure to reconcile the ethereality of the angels with the realism of the future saint's body ... is what makes it one of my favourite paintings' (Lerner 2015, 10), the content of the *Mean Free Path* poems fail to reconcile various tensions between what they seek to depict and the medium they depict them in.

Cut Up, Recombination

The stanzas in *Mean Free Path* produce their confused, unsettled quality through errors, repetitions and discontinuities that have similar features to earlier avant-garde techniques such as the cut-up. Perhaps the most notorious progenitors of the cut-up, William S. Burroughs and Brion Gysin, engaged with the new temporal folds offered by analogue recording materials by cutting up tape recordings and transcribing them or by splicing together newspaper print, producing apparently prophetic juxtapositions. In Burroughs's characteristically incisive prose, 'cut into the present and the Future leaks out' (Burroughs 1963, 43). Indeed, the analogue era encourages the understanding of media as spanning and enclosing a tangible (if disordered) time-space continuum that can be cleaved open.[23] In contrast, the digital edit evokes a different situation for temporality where time-like events are produced by arrangements of data points: what Lerner evokes as 'enabling failures / The little collisions, the path of decay' (40).

Poetics that directly respond to and embrace a condition where textual meaning is generated through forms of (re)arrangement have variously been called generative poetry – 'a literature of which the author does not write the final texts but which only works at the level of the high rank components such as: conceptual models, knowledge rules, dictionary entries and rhetoric definitions' (Balpe 2005); differential texts – 'texts that exist in different material forms, with no single version being the definitive one' (Perloff in Morris and Swiss 2012, 32); and nomadic poetry – 'inscriptions vanish, interfaces multiply, and reception fragments electronic surfaces. There are no statements, only inputs. The result is nomadic poetry, fluid and transitory' (Beiguelman in Morris and Swiss 2015, 285). Bill Seaman (2010) describes as 'recombinant poetics' his own and others' digital artworks that take advantage of new forms of temporality in interaction and mutability. He notes that the right way to understand the audience for these media is in terms of the 'vuser' (viewer/user): 'New technological systems enable participants to glimpse into the actual meaning-related functionalities of media-elements as they are explored through navigation, layering, juxtaposition and interpretation within a specifically authored virtual environment' (Seaman 2010, 159).

What is notable about this description is that it sounds more like a diagnosis of a contemporary literary malaise than a manifesto for avant-garde language practice. Seaman's 'contextualisation, decontextualisation and recontextualisation of media-elements in virtual space' sounds to my ear like a critique of the crisis of truth in current political flows; a situation that Lerner refigures in print as a melancholic stasis. What characterises these poetries is a continued relationship between a source code 'virtual' text, a database of options and the wandering promiscuity of meaning across various versions of an 'actual' surface text produced by calling on this database according to a rule-governed system (as we saw in chapter 1, in the case of J. R. Carpenter's poems). Lerner's work engages with this tradition, but, as I will show, his work complicates the notion of a 'source text' in productive ways and his print iteration is critical of, rather than embracing, the mutable semiotic condition.

Fragmented Standstill

The title poem of *Mean Free Path* consists of two long sequences of stanzas composed from fragmentary phrases that repeat with slight alterations throughout the series, producing a sensation that something has been cut up and rearranged. Indeed, Lerner describes the *Mean Free Path* poems as a kind of 'choose-your-own-adventure', where the audience is brought into a collaborative engagement with meaning-making via the presentation of a series of options. Critics, including Gorin (2010) and Brian M. Reed (2011), have attempted to untangle the possible source texts of *Mean Free Path* from its published version. Gorin suggests it could be a combination of a love poem to his wife, an elegy for a friend who has died and a poem dedicated to his poetic heroes. He says that our experience of reading Lerner's reworking of these sources 'models an ethics of choosing, in which we're bound to acknowledge our decisions as founded on provisional, imperfect norms and knowledge, without entertaining the fantasy that we might be absolved of choice' (2010). But the notion of *Mean Free Path* portrayed in these simplistic interpretations glosses over the mutable nature of the poem's iterative lines: words, phrases and images are not really recombined in the poem but reoccur in different forms. What really evokes the glitch is that, if this is a poem produced by recalling a source text database, something is going wrong in the recall process, and that wrongness is one of the methods the poet chooses to communicate with.

The result is that, rather than a sequence of paths to choose from as we make our way through the poem, alternative versions of paths we have previously taken appear in the road; our 'adventure' is broken up and reimagined as a 'fragmented standstill'. Like this, *Mean Free Path*'s form of recall is subject to the attention deficit thematised in the poems: impressions change as they collide with ideas, structures shift as they collide with iterations, and vice versa. Pattern and expectation become potent tools in this formula. As Lerner observes in an interview:

> The sections [of the book] begin with a modification of the form, but of course this can only be realised retrospectively, after the pattern from which the initial stanza departs has established itself. The exception that proves the rule precedes it. ... So on the one hand this is a kind of loop, an enactment of the repetition it describes – we're back at the beginning. But since the beginning contains the one modification of the formal pattern, a modification we could not initially experience as such, this is a return with a difference, a return to a beginning that now has one of the formal signatures of closure. (in Kunin 2013)

Lerner finds a new kind of poetic language in the busy, disordering operations of new media's paradoxical standstill. The notions of an 'original' image, of closures and beginnings, or of truth and originality, are lost in the networked computational context and *Mean Free Path* is in a distinctively contemporary stasis: one in which the 'infinite mental effort' evoked by Benjamin concerning the daguerreotype becomes a field of confusing, obfuscating potentiality. This reading corresponds to the relationship between past and future that Lerner attributes to the hand-dissolving in Bastien-Lepage's painting. Like a digital glitch, the syntax errors on the surface of Lerner's poems are an excess of pattern, the aesthetics of the poem's contradictions as they distort its content. What distinguishes this method from the cut-up and recombination of the analogue era (and the way some of these ideas have been adopted by 'new media poetics') is that, rather than offering discrete units disordered by process of selection, units *and* modes of choice are in a continual dynamic interplay, reprogramming and correcting one another in our reading.

Data Collisions

The title *Mean Free Path* refers to the journey travelled by a particle or wave before it collides into another in particle physics. Physicists detect the movement of particles through the energy released when they collide. This means that the 'mean free paths' of particles are data-dark moments: the particle is in motion and potent with information that will only be realised on its subsequent collision. This is a fitting analogy for the 'reading paths' of a book whose lines do not register a semantic impact until they are thought through later configurations. The hidden potentiality of semantic interference in the reading process is hinted at persistently through figures in the poem:

> Particles bombarding gold foil or driving rain
> It's the motion, not the material, not the nouns

> But the little delays (Lerner 2010, 25)

The stanzas in *Mean Free Path* fizz in messy – what we might call multi-momentary – moments of the kind we perform in the digital age; the frayed ends of its lines indicate their provisional, depleted nature. They are only ever a statistically possible rendering of the reality they allude to. Likewise, in the poem's ostensibly narrative world, lovers' conversations that are abruptly cut off and returned to from new angles imply that the poem's subjects are distracted, only partially in each other's company: 'I promised I would never / Tell me, whose hand is this' (Lerner 2010, 11).

Asked to elaborate on the relation of the virtual and the ideal in his 2012 interview with Tao Lin, Lerner puts the emphasis on interaction and process:

> BL: It's not that the poet has something inside him he wants to express (which is one model of lyric poetry), something that would just be there if he left it alone, but that poetry is an attempt to figure – with the irreducibly social materials of language – possibilities that have not yet been actualised.
>
> BLVR: But it fails?
>
> BL: Yeah, but a failure can be a figure, can signify. (Lin 2012)

Thought of as signifying failures, the images and statements that make up Lerner's poem negatively figure the media condition; that is, they render an excess (of information) as lack (of coherence) in their gaps and aporia.

Perhaps resonant with the way the gaps and aporia figure the injuries to Bergvall's jaw in 'About Face' discussed in chapter 1, the failures in Lerner's poem are in fact subject matters turned into a kind of textural error. That is, the topics of the poem are present in the form of absences.

> And that's elegy. I know I am a felt
> This is the form where my friend is buried
> Effect of the things that I take personally (56)

The existential doubt expressed by Lerner in this final stanza is connected to the poets' view of the radical impoverishment of language by capital: 'I know that I can't touch her with the hand / That has touched money' (56). He invokes eighteenth-century economist Adam Smith's 'invisible hand' (a figure used in his book *The Wealth of Nations* [1776]): the only hand that can 'touch money'. Rather than touching, entities in Lerner's work, like money and language, and like glitching media, interact by describing and describe by interacting in a kind of shared world of processing. Distances between things, in this case, are at once collapsed and irreducible, and are subject to 'competing forms of closure' in the present. This is also a visual motif for the poem, in which things are dynamically interacting but always at a remove from one another.

Lerner selects moments of clarity in the poem to emphasise the importance of what is apparently not there. Like a sheet of gold foil, the poet's gaze is speckled with gleaming pixels as though it is dissolving into the machine, composed of flickering units that shine and vanish: skin is 'glitter-flecked' (10), or speckled and fading, 'stone-washed', there is 'glass in her hair' (32), and the ear also is open to a cascading fizzing quality as though meanings are only partially arriving from another state, half-appearing statements that hover on the surface of actualisation. The data world is of course also ever present in its absence: 'Wave after wave of information breaks over us / Without our knowledge' (14). (Waves imply a complex but fragile relation between component parts and their movement; what is a wave, after all, without a material to run through?) For this reason, birdsong and applause also appear frequently: both composed of countless discrete moments but apprehended – if at all – as a confused whole. Birdsong is 'a little machine for forgetting' (46), while applause is a reflection of surfaces, simultaneously celebrating and dissolving the possibility of being understood.

> Each of us must ask herself
> Why am I clapping? The content is announced
> Through disappearance, like fireworks. (14)

> How it falls apart if read aloud, or falls
> What we might call its physics
> Together like applause, a false totality
> Scales (56)

Like the image of hissing foil fizzing with 'little delays', birdsong and applause are collisions that are analogous to the irritations Ernst senses in digital images. They echo Benjamin's assertion that subliminal shocks from the environment (the crowd that has disappeared from Daguerre's image of the Paris street) form the basis for a literary texture. It is at the level of minute interactions and subliminal temporal shifts registering as a pattern that the aesthetic of glitch poetics is realised: the tiny temporal processes of the microchip that threaten and sustain the flows of media, or a billion smartphone users uploading texts to the network in any single moment, translated into a figure for how humans relate *in* and *to* a world which is increasingly entangled with code-like temporal irritations.

Code and the Cognitive Artwork

Adorno notoriously expressed frustration with the withheld quality of Benjamin's work on Baudelaire and Paris, asking about the lack of development of Benjamin's primary concerns, 'Is this "material" that can wait patiently for interpretation without being consumed by its own aura?' (Adorno correspondence in Benjamin 2003, 100). In contradiction, Adorno's own approach to immanent critique demands an unsettling, rule-breaking antagonism that will decouple and release the grip in which it is held. When Adorno characterises the stasis inherent in Benjamin's philosophy, the effects of which we see in Lerner's compositional process, as 'Medusan' (Helming 2003), he is criticising the way that Benjamin wants to make living things historical, 'petrifying' them at a remove from the present in order to release their significance. As we have seen, Benjamin's is not a simple historicity, but nonetheless, for Adorno (and so also for Sutherland), poetry and philosophy require a kinetic purchase on the material world that contrasts with Benjamin's approach by specifically addressing and engaging in the accelerated instabilities of modernity's interplay of 'progress and regress' (Helming 2003). This idea is tangibly revitalised by the contemporary context: in the way codes act in the world today in 'the gap between word and force, and logic and praxis is effectively effaced' (Gauthier 2018, 65).

Rather than the static dialectical image, the dynamic proposition of Sutherland's poetry can be thought through Adorno's notion of the 'cognitive artwork'. 'Cognitive artwork' refers to the autonomous qualities of a work, as it processes and communicates truth in a way that exceeds the author's purpose and the manner of its reception. As Simon Jarvis, a (now disgraced)[24] theorist and poet of the Cambridge School who has written on Sutherland's work, comments in his critical introduction to Adorno: 'Works of art, for Adorno, are not merely inert objects, valued or known by the subject; rather, they have themselves a subjective moment because they are themselves cognitive, attempts to know' (Jarvis 1998, 96). As Jarvis states, art objects cannot 'know' or 'do' in the traditional sense, but Adorno is instead suggesting that a complete reading of an art object must take into account the way that elements and materials act on each other as part of the way they work upon the audience and the time of their reception. Adorno attributes the cognitive capacity of artworks to their 'linguistic character', as characterised by Jarvis here:

> The elements of language, morphemes or phonemes and the lexical items which they constitute, are not atoms of fixed meaning which are then simply added up to produce a sum total of meaning, but are variably meaningful, and meaningful only in their relation to other morphemes or phonemes. In an analogous way, Adorno argues, works of art organise elements which have no fixed or essential meaning in themselves into a meaningful relation. They depend on such relations for their eloquence. (103)

This characterisation seems to evoke Lerner's Benjaminian compositional tactics, in which the components of poetry flock and orient awaiting meaningfulness, but Adorno's ideal form differs from that seen in Lerner's churning, contingent poems. Rather than the chance 'shock' encounter of the dialectical image, Adorno 'wants a theory of a complex truth in which apophatic, endeetic and moral-practical moments' are *forced* into a determinate, orchestrated shape (114).

In the following section, I will examine how the cognitive artwork operates as a kind of organising or structural impulse in Sutherland's response to the digital condition. Rather than an ontology of the digital image that stops at the screen, this interpretation relies on understanding code as emphatically effective in the world. Executable code does not contain or store its meanings, but rather enacts them on human and machinic subjects; faltering code and faltering cognition alike have potential in this context. My reading explores the resonance between what Sutherland describes as 'the power of the unfamiliar thing to make knowledge ... become wrong' and the proposition of glitch art that error can inform a new 'interaction gestalt' (Menkman 2011).

The Odes to TL61P

The Odes to TL61P is a book-length series of five odes ostensibly addressed to an obsolete Hotpoint machine part. Cutting sharply between polemical prose, tightly banded metre and fragment forms, each of the odes flickers at the edge of their ode-hood, as Sutherland plays with the limits of what is aesthetically acceptable or even comprehensible. Although this aggressive approach to form is not unique to Sutherland's work, what is notable is that the 'wrongness' of his poems has a distinctively contemporary texture analogous to code that makes it readable as a glitch work.

Sutherland is associated with the Cambridge School, an avant-garde group of poets known for their linguistic impenetrability. Indeed, in many ways, the tactics of *TL61P* are familiar to the conventions of the Cambridge poets – the syntactical strangeness, the linguistically rendered politics and the tendency to critically rework normative rhetorical or literary devices. However, unlike the Cambridge School, the tenor of this book is startlingly unguarded, even naive. For example, the line 'One of your last texts said you wanted to kiss my soul. I fall in an infinite sheet of light' (Sutherland 2013, 60) is too kitsch for a Cambridge School hardened by modernist principles and would perhaps be more at home in the performance poetry scene or an Insta poet's stream. This tendency to embed lines that are 'not at home' is deliberate; a poem working outside of its default settings. I want to draw out the particular ways Sutherland's engagement with, yet refusal of, extant defaults for literature operates in relation to the necessary conflicts of computer code as it administers our emotional, social and political lives.

Sutherland's glitchy lyric language oscillates not between the virtual and actual, as with Lerner's, but between the 'logic and praxis' (Gauthier 2018, 65) of the linguistic statement – its ability to argue for what it seeks to enact and the collapse into malfunction that is the inevitable consequence of this action in the face of poetry's place in the world. Sutherland frequently pushes beyond the logic and praxis of code, against the 'impotence and inertia' of poetic language (Tamplin 2015) in these poems. As a result, what the poem is doing and saying is subject to an interference pattern with the personal, technical and political contingencies that allow it to be said:

> Who the fuck I am now speaking to or at or for
> or not at this moment is compensation for being
> completed into a circle resigned to resume the
> first square the first on the entire board and is

> listening there, afloat and spent yet lost in streaks to the opening night ... the abolition of capital is the social revolution: state again this single fact, in too deep for any scar; in the end, which is right now, looming over a motto executed in the Ottoman style of rococo circumlocution in liberal sex jargon recited by Eriphile (Sutherland 2013, 9)

As we can see in this early passage, the oscillation between praxis and logic in *TL61P* expresses itself as a tension between Sutherland's interior doubts and conflicts and his desire to provoke conflict in us, and the exterior 'noise' of corporate and consumer capitalism.

Forkbomb

In a process called 'compiling', human-readable 'high level' code is turned into 'lower level' machine runnable code and the ones and zeros that coincide with the switching of transistors in microchips. As with the compression and decompression taking place within the digital image, the pervasiveness of compiling means that the language of computers is always a process of arbitration between human-meaningful and machine-actionable codes. The corruptions of register in *TL61P* highlight their affinity with this new temporal irritation of language, through errors that similarly perform an oscillation between the readable and executable: that is, between 'What a poem is and what it does' (Sutherland 2013, 54).

TL61P 1 opens with an apparently scrambled or encrypted fragment: 'dusters wrapt in itching flame, streaked in limbic cloud / pt in itching l6 / blue sky on the setting water, nod til / made to still, remade in onward chains?' (Sutherland 2013, 13). These halfway-meaningful phrases are apparently on their way to being injunctions; caught in an in-between state, they appear corrupted or perhaps uncompiled, suggesting there is a kind of cypher, a logical symbolic problem unsolved in the work.

In fact, Sutherland frequently posits injunctions to the reader that resemble mathematical workings ('a power set of a subset'), alongside command-line instructions to move back and forth across the text prompts ('start again', 'now go back to the start') in order to de-cypher this work. Clues as to the apparently banal title of the poem, and ways of decoding what it means, are paired with injunctions to go back and read again, and therefore enter into a loop. Instead of being a source for information that allows us to progress, these parts of the odes accumulate their tensions in our subliminal cognitive buffer, placing elements of our mental capacity out of order inside recursive attempts to define the subject until it (or we?) become overburdened. In the section excoriating petty bureaucrats, the poem itself appears to crash:

> Giddy detestation of senior liquidity managers, strong aversion to strategy consultants, deep disgust at lead auditors, growing impatience with industry relations directors .... waning displeasure at heads of decision support – irredeemable

> illness of disposition towards regulatory affairs consultants. (Sutherland 2013, 40)

The observation that the poem can crash tips us back towards the genealogy of critical art practices that tactically produce glitches in a computer to expose or interrogate its underlying workings. In particular, the 'forkbomb': a short section of code that, when working correctly, gradually disables the computer system that is running it. Examples include an elegant forkbomb constructed purely of ASCII symbols by Jaromil, quoted here in its entirety: ':(){ :|:& };:'. If these symbols are entered into a Unix command line window, the computer will crash as it eats up its memory by making copies of itself. Jaromil suggests, in fact, that his forkbomb is an example of experimental poetry:

> In considering a source code as literature, I am depicting viruses as poésie maudite, giambi against those selling the Net as a safe area for a bourgeois society. The relations, forces and laws governing the digital domain differ from those in the natural. The digital domain produces a form of chaos – sometimes uncomfortable because unusual, although fertile – to surf thru: in that chaos viruses are spontaneous compositions, lyrical in causing imperfections in machines made to serve and in representing the rebellion of our digital serfs. (Jaromil 2002)

Jaromil frames his literary code as an exemplar of a disruptive linguistic form and connects the forkbomb to

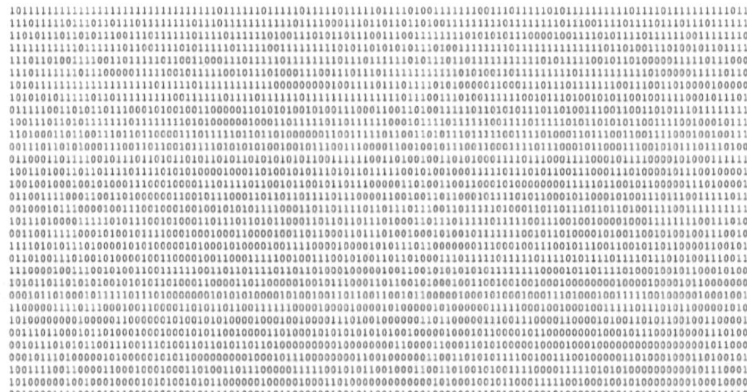

Fig. 13. Screenshot of the computer output from Alex McLean's 'forkbomb', 2001. Used with permission.

its tradition. This echoes Giorgio Agamben's depiction of poetry itself as 'a linguistic operation which renders language inoperative by deactivating its communicative and informative functions in order to open it to a new possible use' (Agamben 2007, 140). What is important here is how the operation and inoperativity of machines, language and humans oscillate in the poem.

Alex McLean's forkbomb renders the computer that runs it inoperative by commanding it to run a single calculation process that branches out to more and more subprocesses, each launching their own subprocesses, and so on, until – depending upon the capabilities of the computer – the system's resources are exhausted and it crashes, outputting a sequence of zeros and ones (fig. 13). The Transmediale website says of this work, 'the pattern in which these data are presented can be said, in one sense, to represent the algorithm of the code, and, in another way, to represent the operating system in which the code is running. The result is an artistic expression of a system under stress' (cited in Weiß 2015). In terms evocative of Sutherland's descriptions of poetry's tension between 'impotence and inertia', Geoff Cox describes how the forkbomb, as a proliferation of endless loops operating on themselves, 'neatly corresponds with a dialectical understanding of the inherent antagonism between internal and external factors, oscillating between what is possible and what actually exists' (Cox and McLean 2012, 44). The 0 and 1 'poem' output by the computer as it runs McLean's forkbomb shows this oscillation in action.

Forkbombs employ a facet of coding called 'subroutines': smaller routines that run and provide input data to the central one, resulting in a programme running processes simultaneously, one nested within another until they overwhelm the computer's executable or storage memory. Resonating with the logic of the forkbomb, 'objectification and violence' (Lerner 2010) become tools in Sutherland's composition process. He suggests that the shifts of logic demanded by breakages within the poem offer analogous transformations to how we consider our role in bureaucratic structures.

The code TL61P belongs to a hotpoint dryer.
You'll find nothing if you look
it up through the sky in the screen, the vault
of exchangeable passion

...

Nobody can take away the word for it:
love, the provisional end until death;

TL61P its unconditional perfected shadow
Opposite; Now go back to the start.
(Sutherland 2013, 24)

The codes in this book, Sutherland suggests in this extract, contain their own purpose, but each time we encounter what this purpose is, it becomes lost in the interference patterns of memory and image: 'These odes are an only deficiently reorderable anagram whose letters don't all move laughed at during oral sex' (Sutherland 2013, 11). These injunctions together produce the sensation that Sutherland and the reader are both nested in runtimes rather than reading and writing the poem, and that our inevitable failure to keep up with the poem has implications for the possible and actual existing worlds of codified reality.

Wrong Poetry

The rhetorical mode of kitsch or the commonplace, mixtures of bureaucratic language, advertising speak and assorted ephemera 'spam' that is the background noise of contemporary communication combine with political and cultural theory in *TL61P* in ways that problematise one another. For Sutherland, the aim of the algorithmic poem-as-game is not to absorb and occupy the reader in the production of truth, as with Lerner's *Mean Free Path*, but rather to force us to crash out, making our persisting understandings – of literature, of political reality – 'become wrong'. Sutherland emphasises this in his essay 'Wrong Poetry', where he cites Adorno's intent for art to contain a power: the 'power of the unfamiliar thing to make knowledge, or the intellectual, "wish to be right" ... [and furthermore to] make knowledge, or the intellectual, become wrong' (Sutherland 2010, 766).

Indeed, for Adorno the weight and capacity of the modern artwork are diametrically opposed to the forms of truth evident in it and the acceptability of its appearance. Adorno uses the example of Beckett's plays:

> Everyone shudders at them, and yet no-one can persuade himself that these eccentric plays and novels are not about what everyone knows but no-one will admit. ... [They] ... deal with a highly concrete historical reality: the abdication of the subject. Beckett's Ecce Homo is what human beings have become. ... Here every commitment to the world must be abandoned to satisfy the ideal of the committed work of art. (Adorno 1997 [1970], 86)

In 'Wrong poetry', Sutherland gives an example of a committed poetic wrongness from Wordsworth's poem 'The Thorn'. He cites a peculiar couplet that the poet's contemporaries decried but that Wordsworth himself asserted readers 'should like': 'I've measured it from side to side / 'Tis three feet long and two feet wide' (Wordsworth, quoted in Sutherland 2010, 765). These lines, Sutherland says, are among the best Wordsworth has written because they are ill-suited to the poetry of the day, and 'the difficulty of liking them should be felt as strongly and unbearably as anyone could feel it' (765).[25] Sutherland doubles down on Wordsworth's literalness in his odes by dedicating the entire work to a now-obsolete washer dryer.

Much that appears wrong in *The Odes to TL61P* is due to the way register unsettles how the poem should be read: Ancient Greek references give way to contemporary economic analyses; metaphorical hierarchies and narrative voice frequently crumble under the pressure of the extended, bewilderingly complex syntax; and, throughout, apparent typos and syntax errors litter the text. Some of the errors seem accidental, while others display a kind of virtuosic control and complexity, perhaps suggesting that the poem is captured halfway through encryption, as though being compiled into a higher- or lower-level language. In this extract, the aposiopesis evokes someone under the control of multiple runtime processes of recall and calculation:

> Impersonated love absconds to
> scapegoat paradise.f
>
> Smile out a window. Shimmering under
> tenderness, sex and rage; the
>
> vertical limit is past the unlimited average, in the
> everything aisle.
>
> (Sutherland 2013, 23)

Echoing the subject-level wrongness implied in the title, *TL61P*'s 'internal' linguistic disunity continues in this 'absolutely literal' manner, producing friction between what a poem can and can not contain. In the next section, I want to look at Sutherland's contemporary reconsideration of another historical methodology for combining things in syntactically wrong ways: parataxis.

Parataxis of Form

Parataxis allows grammatically incommensurable lines to be combined in quick succession, producing a series that is 'harsh as it is flowing' (Adorno 1991 [1958], 136-38). Parataxis is a form of early textual glitch, similar to the cut-up, emphasising the slippage and interference between lines. Adorno suggests that poets can use parataxis to exceed the semantic bounds of linguistic structures. In his essay 'Parataxis: On Hölderlin's Late Poetry', Adorno says that the German poet uses parataxis to transgress and exceed the territory of poetic form. For Adorno, Hölderlin's parataxis operates similarly to Wordsworth's 'absolute literalness', compelling the reader to engage in what is difficult to assimilate about the text. By working outside of 'proper' grammar, parataxis forced contemporaneous readers to acknowledge and question their cognitive adherence to grammatical form as the arbiter of what can and cannot be said. This is the challenge also that Sutherland wants to set for his readers, but he is rightly suspect whether a technique that was effective in the nineteenth century because it was startling then could be effective now.

Since the Romantic era, parataxis has been thoroughly assimilated into conventional poetics of the modernist textual experiment, conceived of as a media-inspired method for collage and accelerating verse forms into staccato 'free' verse and clipped phrases more akin to newspaper or telegraph bulletins. As Adorno states regarding forms that themselves become formulaic: 'Such works drift to the brink of indifference,

... into idle repetition of formulas now abandoned in other art-forms, into trivial patterns' (Adorno 1997 [1970], 87). The disjunctive effect of breaking lines in this fashion has been watered down by their similarity to forms of communication that have succeeded the newspaper and telegraph. Indeed, in the approach of Lerner, there is a numbing effect to the technique that makes the language more porous and 'fuzzy' than disjunctive. A Twitter or Facebook feed is a paratactic phenomenon many of us read several times a day. Interestingly, the display algorithms deployed on every social media posting operate at different, more complex, logics than the posts' appearance in a series implies – deriving potent psychological effects by linking and mixing current and historical materials with predictive behaviours. Indeed, the most unsettling aspects of the social media 'feed' are not so much the juxtaposing of units, but rather ways in which they are hybridised, personalised and woven from one browser window to another, tracking and feeding our desires in an addictive, habit-forming loop. The scales of online language flow-disjunctions are larger (to do with ordering and processes happening across different operating system windows) and smaller (more subtle and fine-grained) than those of the analogue era, and they require a different mode for language also. The comparison to Lerner and Sutherland's work is instructive.

The disjunctions of parataxis in the social media feed, lists of non-sequiturs, syntactically incomplete new-news from every conceivable kind of corporate or corporeal entity have become the norm, producing a torpid, trance-like, compulsive effect in the reader. The presence of this atmosphere can also be detected in several of the 'internet age' novels I write through in chapter 3, and speak to a particular class (or classless) condition from which Lerner writes. Sutherland's response to the media-sphere, in comparison to Lerner's, is tangibly, texturally difficult. A sense of struggle pervades the reading of his work in a way that recalls earlier ideas around parataxis, but it also pushes this mode into a method for embodied struggle that is distinctively at odds with the contemporary.

The difference from Lerner's work perhaps indicates that Sutherland feels the habitual, languid experience of the internet scroll exists in direct conflict with other aspects of the digital age: the material struggle with increasingly complex meshes of financial, mental health and political difficulties that also characterise this time. Rather than writing sympathetically with the online environment, Sutherland's poetry responds to the internet as a 'harsh ... flow' rubbing up against the embodied and cognitive task of coping with the world. His work embodies the harshly fluid qualities of the internet by invoking the 'crash' alongside his new deployment of parataxis as a form and metaphor.

In an interview with *Blackbox Manifold*, Sutherland states that he rejects the salient default of parataxis to further pressurise his own writing into different, less formulaic, forms of disjunction:

> [I]t suddenly felt to me as though experience had to be crammed into a space, compressed between inelastic limits, stuffed down – put under the maximum possible pressure *as if from above*. It came to feel to me as though line endings in versification, though they worked as pivots or sources of tension and pressure, also sometimes worked as release valves and as exits from or exonerations of the tension of syntax. I suddenly felt as though my writing couldn't accommodate those exits, that it needed to be totally blocked in. In the *Odes*, it still also felt essential that at moments writing would erupt out–whether into what you fairly call a kind of doggerel verse form, or whether into verse which still tries to be jagged and uncertain; it erupts out into various types of versification. (in Tamplin 2015)

The disjunctions of parataxis are not calculated features for harsh flow anymore but rather 'default' pressure-release valves for poetry. Sutherland suggests that by resisting this default towards fragmentation, other pressures build in his work. According to Sutherland, the refusal of the line break forces him to find a new form of language disjunction that is appropriate to the technical and political fractures our time. As he says, 'It's all about living under the present pressure of what it means right now to be in the world, from the most inward atom to the furthest outer reaches of social relations that I can see or imagine' (in Tamplin 2015). The most striking aspect of this pressurised combination of disjunctive elements in *TL61P* is how the book flickers and jerks between verse and prose lineation in ways that make both feel wrongly applied, with no real sense of when or why a particular form is selected. This is parataxis, but *with* form rather than *as* form. Adorno also suggested that parataxis can be effective on different scales within the lyric: 'It is not only the micrological forms of serial transition in a narrow sense, however, that we must think of as parataxis. As in music, the tendency takes over larger structures' (Adorno 1991, 132).

An example of the parataxis of form: in 'Ode to TL61P 1', part 1.1 is a single sentence of unbroken prose which extends for four pages in an emphatic mode – 'Each time you unscrew the head the truths burn out... to recycle the joy it brings, the power set, of a subset, of a powerset, of a sex power,/' (Sutherland 2013, 7-10) – before breaking into a lineated, more lyrical free verse ('suburbanites of backstreet Uberbollywood in flower/ for the first time since you not only die/ at all since how could you not; biting' [11]), and a series of six-line rhyming stanzas ('But if that will keep its grip/ in there since not exhausted from/ without a light dissolves to rip/ and shine again was all I am' [11]), and then rhyming quatrains that flicker between hymnal and kitsch ('Our glaring end annuls in light/ what fire on the faded past/ remains whose shadow cannot last/ as you burn away in bright' [12]). These six pages jam together different conceits and tones in such a disjunctive way that they contradict the formal synthesis the parataxis of lyric poem is supposed to allow (Jackson and Prins 2014, 353).

Rather than with a single working, flowing lyric, we are presented with a flow that is the result of a compounded seriation. It is indeed as though the poem (and its reader) are put under pressure, to the point that the poem's structure cannot contain them, so it is 'forced' into a leaks and splurges of form and content. As with the syntactical splurges of Erica Scourti's predictive text poems and YHCHI's 'clean glitch', this work counters the intuitive expectancy that glitched language is fragmented language and confronts us instead with a physical engagement with a leaky poetics. As I have suggested, Sutherland intends this aspect of the poems to be symbolic of the ethically, physically and cognitively pressurised conditions for living outside of poetry.

Kludge

A comparable technique to parataxis in glitch cultures is the *kludge*. Kludging refers to the plugging of incompatible elements to make something work, albeit inefficiently and unconventionally: 'a work around, or a way of temporarily fixing something which is inefficient and will not last, but works in a pinch' (Temkin 2014). As the term's assonance with *sludge* and *mud* implies, the kludge is a process of leaky operation, a space between working and malfunction. Notably, the kludge often pressurises a system into unanticipated outputs. In *Prepared Desktop*, performed at Transmediale festival in 2012, the glitch artist Jon Satrom visibly 'crashes' the Mac desktop interface by overloading it with a kludge of different processes running simultaneously. As the performance starts, Satrom is sharing his desktop with the audience on a screen behind him, and we see the computer prompt him to install a 'plug-in', which he does. As this is loading, multiple other prompts and 'compatibility error' messages begin to appear. Soon the screen is swarming with installation instructions, license agreements, pop-up error boxes, loading icons – all appear layered on top of one another, creating a funny, baffling maelstrom (figs. 14a & b). Alongside the proliferation of windows and alerts, components are pulled apart and stuck together in odd ways; the animation effects of 'spinning' are applied to a window, making it impossible to read; text auto-scrolls and 'beach balls' grow like maximised windows.

Satrom's work takes incompatibility as its subject and method. In *Prepared Desktop*, 'normal use' is eschewed in favour of a potent dysfunctionality: when it glitches, the apparently stable 'unified' Mac OSX operating system is shown to be, in practice, heterogeneous and composed of many moving parts, each leaking and splurging into the next. Satrom's funny glitch-hyperbole creates a new kind of flow: a flow of slippages emerging from the code-unconscious of the software. It satirises the frustrations we have in the moments our machines do not work as intended by compounding errors and turning them into a kind of panicked, twitching celebration of computer refusal.

The same can be said of Sutherland's pressurised implementation of various verse and prose forms, images and tropes inherited from the lyric poetry

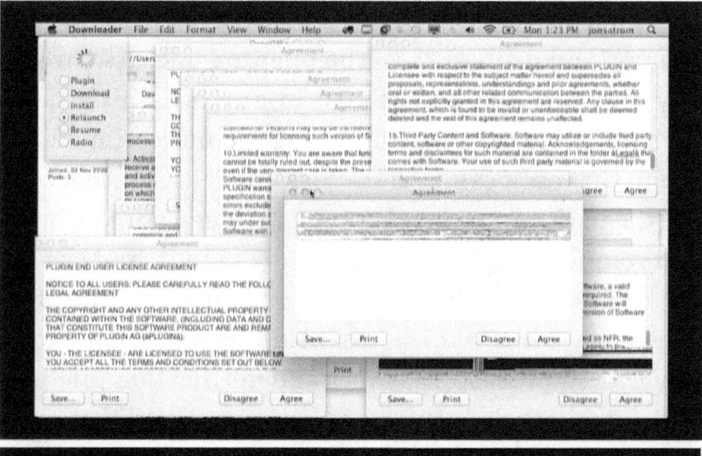

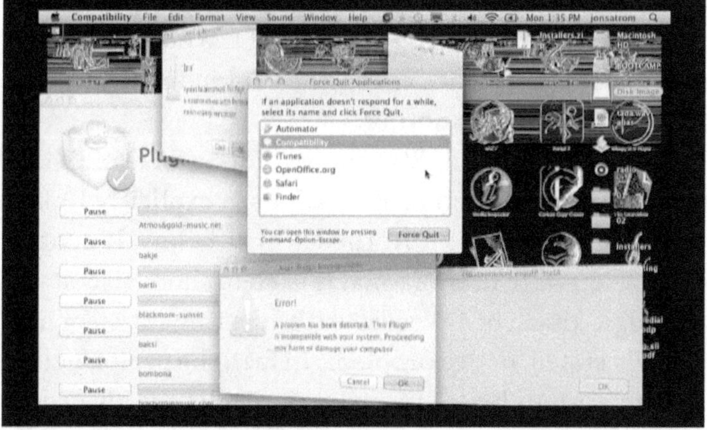

Figs.14a and 14b. Screenshots from Jon Satrom's performance, Prepared Desktop, 2012. Used with permission.

'operating system'. Rather than a carnivalesque celebration of dysfunctionality, though, *TL61P* brings the reader into close contact with a terminal frustration. This can be seen in sections that deploy prose lineation with iambic and rhyming patterns, to the degree that the rhyme scheme gives the impression of being shifted and pushed from without. For example, the forced rhymes and drop-outs in the opening ode: 'As sure as any air must spread the cost of any breathing head thrilled out to cold perfection to keep our estimates so rough that each can lean in close enough...' (Sutherland 2013, 23). Here, the hard rhyme between spread/head and rough/enough of 'perfection' (I read it, 'per-fec-ti-on', adding a syllable so that it scans) accelerates the flow away from 'natural' scansion in ways that evoke the layered processing errors and notification pile-ups in Satrom's work. In such passages, we sense that metronomic form and rhyme schemes are logics that have been applied to the wrong section of the poem as it corrupts, slips and comes apart, each component working in contradiction to another.

Sometimes, the digital context for Sutherland's linguistic overloads and proliferations is explicitly linked to the digital context. In the excerpt below, language from a software user manual is used to short-circuit the nostalgic kitsch of a Wordsworth-like romanticism into a wryly stated 'better problem'. In fact, the performative 'automatic' quality of the excerpt recalls the absurdity of Satrom's glitch performances that turn incompatibility and inoperability into an art form:

> Years of my life wasted on war, depressed and miles away. Je le vis. The menu bar and buttons are displayed above the text fields: The line below shows many product codes; Use the menu bar to choose commands: In addition to the standard menus; File, Edit and View,

> ... activated and deactivated at the point View Toolbar. As for humanity, right now, it can be ignored or converted into a better problem. (Sutherland 2013, p.33)

Sutherland's tangling of registers in these moments is uncannily evocative of the frustrations of digital environments: the parallel processing of the cognitive labourer who clicks links, opens tabs and shifts between windows, all the while in fear for their job; or the rapid shifting of algorithmic processes as they oscillate between crashing and restabilising beneath a glossy exterior.[26] As noted in the introduction, the condition of a system working at its limits, where multiple layers of parallel processing produce unsettling and disjunctive effects as they become partially apparent to us in glitches, is the new normal. Codes continually deal with their own crises in the process of administering our relations, and these crises are tangible as a trace as we sublimate them. We can interpret Sutherland, as we can Satrom and numerous other glitch artists, as producing an 'immanent critique' of the patterns and preconceived schemata of systems. For these glitch artists, there are radical opportunities for alterity embedded in the way the system operates.

Odes and Codes

The ode form is the literary operating system for the *TL61P* poems: the means through which it interfaces with the literary system. It is the ode whose prepackaged forms and tropes Sutherland inherits from

Wordsworth and the ancient Greek poet Pindar, amplifying them and kludging them with contemporary concerns, producing telling malfunctions. The anachronism of the ode offers several fruitful opportunities for Sutherland to distinguish his work from his contemporaries. He also develops a kind of media archaeology of code. In these following sections, I want to look at the echoes of form between odes and codes by looking back at iterations of the ode form that influenced Sutherland, and at how they are code-ified in *TL61P*.

Geoffrey Hartman (1964) describes the way Wordsworth uses the ode-form based around three movements of a strophe (movement), antistrophe (anti-movement) and epode (stand). Hartman highlights how opposing movements of 'flux and reflux' and stasis or 'stand' are embedded in the ode's combination of a tripartite structure and the 'style of thought' that invites reversal:

> The irregular rhythms, a privilege of the ode form, work independently of specific stanza or stage of argument to express the flux and reflux of a mind ... even though each stanza tends to mingle rising and falling rhythms, stanzas III and IV are, as it were, a 'counter-turn' to stanzas I and II, while stanza V is a kind of epode of 'stand' in which the passion seems to level out into a new generalization or withdrawal from personal immediacy. (Hartman 1964, 51)

The combinations of passion, levelling out and withdrawal across the sections of an ode and the way in which they are counter-posed and contradicted in following sections are characteristics that are heightened in Sutherland's kludged versions of this form. As with the tangling and corruption of registers throughout the poem, the overlapping of movements and momentums that characterises Sutherland's adaptation of the ode-form has a flavour that recalls its digital context: code also functions as layers of parallel process, sometimes contradicting each other. As we have seen, Sutherland sees potential in these contradictions and so amplifies them. While tendencies of the ode-form are to contradict and return, in *TL16P* movement and anti-movement are made to coexist, resonating with the way that logic and praxis, run-time and malfunction, coexist in computer codes. There is a clue to Sutherland's approach to the ode's contradictions in his titling: the epode of ode 1.3 doubles as the strophe for section 2, titled in the Roman numeral 'I' – which means meaning that this section oscillates between the standing still and counter-turning function, arguing and providing its own counterargument.

Sutherland's work also consciously cites an earlier form of the ode in ways that productively resonate with code conventions. As classicist Leslie Kurke (2013) observes, writing about the productive 'executable-like' aspect of the Greek poet Pindar's odes, the poet used metaphors that 'shifted rapidly' within a line, producing a fizzing density in the poems, which was designed as an active component. As Kurke puts it, through the ode Pindar 'secures the present victory for the house and "brings home" the memory of past victories' (2013, 21) by making the poem's language exceed its referential function. She gives the following example: 'Check your oar and swiftly fix the anchor in the earth from the prow, as a defense against the rocky reef. For the peak of encomiastic hymns flits from topic to topic like a honeybee' (Pindar, quoted in Kurke 2013, 10). The metaphors here proliferate and overlap in illogical ways, deriving an affective sensation from that error. Kurke argues that it is precisely through the looping and overlapping of such images that Pindar's poetry transcends normative language use, so abstract concepts such as memory and victory can be brought into a specific geographical location as executables.

The *TL61P* odes are a faltering, faulty step-by-step procedure that 'runs' its virus-like error effects on the person that reads them. No matter how emphatic Sutherland's argument, we are continually crashing out of its runtime, being caught in flickering, irresolvable metaphor-logics, or forced to read again where certain sections push a reading forward at a rate that is inimical to the semantic complexity of its content. In doing so, readers are invited to consider how machine-like the demands made on us by capitalism are; the poem asserting an analogy between the code-like operations of poetry that crashes and the bureaucratic procedures that seek code-like control over citizens. Letting us fail or crash out of the odes, Sutherland seeks to extrapolate the possibility of alterity through error into our relationship to the political status quo.

Wrongness and Confession

Beyond the title and forms of stylistic disjunction, the most startling example of Sutherland's attempt in *TL61P* to interface the personal and political is the deployment of the author's own sexual experiences as a child with another child. Childhood sexuality is positioned in *TL61P* as having such a powerful ambiguity that it glitches the languages of social 'care' and interpersonal 'love', and is imagined as an existential glitch from which a new kind of adult romance could emerge: 'I felt myself become a hole. I now think I emerged as a hole for him; I now emerge as a hole for you' (Sutherland 2013, 62). Childhood sexual activity is a confusing area for existing judicial and social frameworks, where it is problematic and difficult to apportion blame (Craig 2020). It is also a phenomenon in which the ethics of children and the adults responsible for them are entangled with image and information flows, particularly children's exposure to sexual imagery and the kinds of sensational reporting that echo it.

Sutherland uses this encounter as a focal point to demand we rethink – and refuse – the basis of current socialised relationships. This is the major gambit in his work. The failure of Sutherland's attempt to name and universalise the feelings of an irreducibly personal encounter (one that is objectively and unambiguously wrong both by law and social convention, yet understood as right from the point of view of its child-narrator), and the way it glitches against our own sense of propriety, become a demanding synecdoche for the failures of the poem to free its audience from enclosed political possibilities. In the most startlingly candid moments of the odes, the writing reaches a pitch where the command-line principles of its early phases combine with the 'innocent' yet 'mature' desire of the early sexual encounter. The poem is jammed with the sensationalised violence and shame inherent in the media-sphere to become a glitching speech act, a judicial directive oscillating through the romantic register: 'you are lost, stared at like distant fire through a screwed up eyelid the waxing ode indulged into redundancy of ear; make the love that makes you disappear' (Sutherland 2013, 26):

> we look at each other's parts under the table, Jackie and I, hiding our eyes in the heads we come with, so as by the beautiful misidentification of excitement with fear to remain children forever, ... I haven't seen her since then; she may be tied up in a Fallujah basement in nothing but a hood, toe-separators and a face dildo; but whatever she is thrilled by now, and whatever she lives in fear of, I trust in truth that somewhere beneath all the real objects there still shines to her distraction the first image of the male genitals I gave her, wrongly flickering, spitting blanks, preserved in trailing clouds, tiny and perfect, the origin and corner of my love. (26)

The attempt to clearly state autobiographical events of this nature in the poems and pin down their meaning is haunted, perhaps tortured, by its internalised responsibility to find political effects, and by Sutherland's self destructive, self-defeating, violently sexual language – which, as he has established, is itself a shock-response to exterior pressures. In the *Blackbox Manifold* interview, where Sutherland is challenged to qualify his assertion that the personal confession is a political action, he refers to figural and literal pressures on the writing process:

> It's a pressure of irremediably private psychic history, instinct and unconscious desire and dream, and it's a pressure of the world bearing down on you and pushing you up and erasing you and making you conform and throwing you about, in certain directions or in none, and of showing you the lives of other people who are similarly being erased and being pushed about. For me, it's when poetry allows both of those pressures to be intensified to their maximum that we get something like the possibility of lyric. (in Tamplin 2015)

What is necessary for Sutherland – and here he is echoing Adorno specifically – is that the poem is 'difficult to bear without real loss' (Ferris 2010). Certainly, for some readers, the violence of Sutherland's work will be unacceptable. As with its autobiographical commitments, the poem's glitches seek moments where the 'possibility of the lyric' emerges from conditions that are political precisely because they are unsustainable, exhibiting the language of the point of collapse. *TL61P* is, in this sense, an invocation of failure, whereby reading (and failing to read) Sutherland's performed writing we experience how difficult life should be to articulate and understand.

Conclusion

The way that emotion and politics are combined in the online sphere results in excesses of affect and a mode of kitsch generalisation and affective fakery designed to appeal to a broad audience, serving only to repeat the existing preconceptions of that audience. The appeal of kitsch resides in its formula, its familiarity and its validation of shared sensibilities. Advertising similarly leans on ambiguously emotional content to reify norms in a way that belies product claims for difference and disruption. In online 'filter bubbles' and 'echo chambers', along with the ease of replication – forwarding, retweeting, sharing – the twin appeal of generic and excessively affected content is amplified. The 'real forgery' of kitsch has come to dominate the popular discourse.

Lerner and Sutherland both seek, and I think arrive at in different ways, a manner of address that combines a heightened emotional language with the performativity of embedded vernacular, in a way that invites a reconsideration of our position concerning the overwhelming cognitive pressures of the digital. At the heart of these practices is a concerted realism, which in the next chapter I define as a *media* realism, whereby the authors push language to absorb the subliminal effects of living in a media environment. Comparatively reading their work alongside the codes and codecs that underpin the digital and online experience, I have tried to show that these poets offer modes for the lyric that contrast the kitsch that characterises mainstream intersections of the political and personal with the conventions of advertising. Both poets are searching for a poetic voice that is 'of' the digital but that embodies its most extreme implications in a way that invites reappraisal, rather than further amplified versions of what exists. For Lerner, this reappraisal requires a ghostly hesitancy, a kind of porous aestheticisation of digital textures as feeling; for Sutherland (for whom labour and living conditions are a more immediate concern), the poem evokes an emphatic struggle and difficulty.

In the next chapter, I push the notion of media realism further, suggesting that we can read back into experimental writing to discern aspects of the then-latent technologies that have since become mainstream. Indeed, in the years since the publication of *Mean Free Path* and *Odes to TL61P*, the media sphere could be said to have become more densely glitchy in the modes of these poets. Lerner's attenuated phrases perhaps resemble nothing so much as Donald Trump's notorious deployment of non-sequitur and aposiopesis at his political rallies: a kind of rhetorical technology uniquely suited to the political context of the filter bubble. But they also evoke for me, writing today, the form of tender language interference that I have become used to during a year of a Covid-induced lockdown, when many of my intimate family relations have been conducted at the remove of a screen and a network, autocomplete and auto-captioning, with genuine emotion flattened together into text and gappy speech.

On a different note, Sutherland's densely hybridised language and averaging of register-differentials could be said to condense his sources in a manner akin to artificial intelligence auto-encoders, resulting in the kinds of corruption and monstrous rhetoric that evokes, to me, the writing generated by a poorly trained AI model. But perhaps more pertinently, Sutherland's work gestures towards a future in which political speech and executable language are themselves hybridised into an algorithmic auto-bureaucracy, a deployment of statistics and logic as political expediency that is embodied in the motto of 'follow the science' during the Covid-19 era while the government transitions absurd amounts of wealth and contracts to ill-suited operators: the flows of billions of pounds worth of medical emergency money being channelled to a pub landlord or an off-shore family lawyer in Mauritius could be a conceit from Sutherland's poem. This is the latent quality *TL61P*'s discomforting realism detected in the networks of the 2010s; a politicised executable corrupt and corrupting viral language arriving before its time.

Chapter 3

Proto-Media-Realist Glitch

Literary realism is commonly thought of as a styleless genre in which language is used in a default way to portray life as plainly as possible. But progenitors of the realist novel, such as Honoré de Balzac and Emile Zola, were considered literary innovators during their time. In fact, they thought their work with the novel to be 'experimental' in that it broke with and distorted existing conventions (Hodgson 2019). Furthermore, their literary experiments were closely linked to their days' newest media (Pold 2000). We can short-circuit the gap between experimental and realist fiction today by using glitch poetics, to reopen a lineage of 'media-realist' authors that turn new media encounters into errant literary styles.

As Goriunova and Shulgin have suggested in their work on glitch, the motif of the error as 'unplanned action' is inherent in the realist tradition of literary innovation and response, '[a]s aesthetic principles, chance, unplanned action, and uncommon behaviours were already central to European and Russian literature of the nineteenth century in the work of writers such as Balzac, Flaubert and Dostoyevsky' (Goriunova and

Shulgin 2008, 114). More recently, the unpredictable has returned to our sense of what is real in ways that literature has to account for. In *The Great Derangement,* Amitav Ghosh (2017) argues that the Anthropocene offers up a new and compelling logic for the unplanned action to take a more prominent position in contemporary literature. Ghosh's work suggests that the world amplifies and returns our actions to us in unknowable ways:

> [T]he freakish weather events of today, despite their radically nonhuman nature, are nonetheless animated by cumulative human actions. In that sense, the events set in motion by global warming have a more intimate connection with humans than did the climatic phenomena of the past– this is because we have all contributed in some measure, great or small, to their making. They are the mysterious work of our own hands returning to haunt us in unthinkable shapes and forms. (Ghosh 2017)

Climate change and the accelerations of environmental destruction belie the impression that our human dramas are entirely (even mainly) the result of our own intentions, or the only source of unpredictability.

The unstable modes by which we are abstracted into data-point intersections, which Goriunova (2018) calls 'digital subjects', create additionally insecure narrative environments. Goriunova's concept of the 'digital subject' parallels Ghosh's characterisation of a planet returning our actions to us in ghostly form in that it describes the product of relations of unknowable complexity in which our activities are entangled. Like the planet's climate, we experience and know ourselves today in moments of unplanned action, glitches that cut through the distance between us and our data image, moments when we realise we are connected to flocks of living data or acting entirely without purchase on the material world. Today's climate and media networks are part of the world that realist authors attempt to bring into focus by visualising it through the lens of individual dramas and rendering it as textual style. This means that individuals and their languages are often subject to glitching events, new and hybridised languages, and error-sensations that are different to those of book characters in earlier eras.

The act of writing latent qualities of media as a literary media-realism often precedes these same media expanding their influence and scope. This state of events provides me with a framework to look back at experimental literature from early in the information revolution as *proto*-media-realisms, suggesting that in their particular unreality and unfamiliarity, and precisely because they were manifestly errant in their form at the time of publishing, the resolutely anti-traditional modernist works of Samuel Beckett and James Joyce anticipated the media-induced linguistic accelerations of today. I use the term 'proto-media-realisms' to refer to experimental literature in which authors develop latent media tendencies into a style that captures the essence of mainstream media experience in later generations.

Raymond Williams (1977) described his process of literary analysis as reading for 'structures of feeling', in which new forms of social structure can be felt emerging as gaps and differences from the literary mainstream of its day. In their focus on texture and disjunction, glitch poetics offer frequent opportunities for such feeling-structures to be encountered, and so contain opportunities for literary readings of the way media's meanings come to shape our social norms. One boundary project that puts pressure on realism and experimentalism is class and its relationship to workplaces. The particular work depicted in the 'internet novels' of Tao Lin, Sheila Heti and, more recently, Lauren Oyler means that the media climate is rendered in a relatively benign form of error where the world is characterised more by boredom than struggle. There are different kinds of embodied media intensity for working-class people, requiring different literary and linguistic styles.

Proto-media-realist authors often over-articulate the effects of current media environments. In doing so, they pre-empt the results of media becoming more intensely dominant over personal and social experience. One aspect of the apparent exaggeration found in proto-media-realisms is that it offers an opportunity to discern gaps in the impressions left by todays acknowledged literary realities: proto-media-realisms, along with speculations on what media can become, are often responding to the lesser-known, lesser-written challenges and intensities of today's working-class lives.

As Fran Lock (2021) has observed, 'the social conditions and particular pressured contexts that produce innovation' are more intensely felt by working-class people. Literature production may less frequently reflect this group because of social and artistic boundaries to their writing, but their experience now can be projected as a commonplace for all in the future. Though this writing may not be well represented, I will show (agreeing with scholars such as Lock) that there are clear ingredients for language practices that address these pressurised contexts – and a strong line of media-realist activity to read it alongside.

Glitches in the lives of people lower down the social scale are more likely to be moments when they fail to keep up or think straight in the context of language technologies that are monitoring and temporalising their labour. Working-class or ethnic vernaculars are also often considered as kinds of error. In discourse analysis, it is common to observe a social *faux pas* in the working-class speaker who does not modulate their language for particular occasions. Peter Middleton (2016) has observed that the British avant-garde poetry tradition can be distinguished from its American version because it commonly works through a programme for 'proper' and 'improper' language. What interests me is how media-realist literature has absorbed this tendency towards formal modulation of language, how media form another – perhaps more stringent – set of default languages to which the working class are expected to conform, and what kinds of language error emerge from this condition. This concern converges with my enquiry into the contemporary workplace, which I suggest is more mediatised, more saturated by digital audio-visual cultures and data flows the lower down the wage scale one looks. One author who appears to write into the gap for experimental, working-class, media-saturated writing is David Peace. At the end of this chapter, I look at his fictionalised account of the miner's strike in 1984, in particular his use of omnipresent radio playlist pop music, finding in it a proto-media-realism that anticipates the cognitive intensities of today's online environment – and that resonates with the work of more recent 'posthuman' fictions.

Realism: Demystification and Defamiliarisation

Literary realism was initially a technical effect of existing literary forms – letters, diaries, journalism, genre fiction – being kludged into modes of operation that were attuned to a social and technological moment. The industrial revolution and the associated accelerations of urbanisation and mass and long distance communication were the contexts that demanded a new literary form, pressurising the space between existing forms and producing a hybrid realist novel. This means that the realist novel is a technical innovation underpinned by a spirit of radicalism and hybridity, resulting in a porousness that we rarely associate with the default literary style of today, and certainly not the formal purity with which realist 'literary fiction' is separated from other novel genres, let alone different disciplinary fields of discovery. In fact, today, the realist literature impulse is possibly better found in its hybrids with other artistic and cultural forms.

As Andrew Hodgson has observed, Zola connected the realist project from its beginnings to an 'experimental' approach to the novel that first of all prompted its audience to question its medium and that sought to problematise the reader-writer relationship. Zola and other authors of this line of 'experimental realism' aimed to use the novel's internal space as an 'experiential synecdoche' for the historic changes in 'beyond-text, interactions of human and social and culture and the world' (Hodgson 2020, 77). The realist novel therefore emerged in contradiction to romantic literature. It inherited ideas of 'classical' art as a form that sought to confront its audience with a sometimes shocking or salacious, sometimes morally grey, and certainly direct, view of 'things as they are', in forms and textures that were difficult to absorb without questioning or adapting a reading approach.

There is here a double resonance between literary realism and the realisms of the glitch: 'experimental realism' glitches literature by kludging pre-existing literary forms into one another, forming new kinds of readerly approach. It offers a direct encounter with the workings 'beneath the surface' of appearances, using the internal, linguistic workings of literature to present an encounter with 'things as they are'. Echoing this interpretation, Frederic Jameson (2013) suggests two aspects to literary realism that have received a different emphasis throughout its history. Firstly, Jameson says, early literary realism (associated with authors such as Balzac and Zola in France, for example) was focussed on the 'demystification' of bourgeois subjectivity and the 'painful cancellation of tenaciously held illusions' promulgated through romantic fiction's idealism, or classical art's emphasis on grand themes. This 'negative social function' recalls the various iterations of glitch effects on the interaction gestalt that I have described in this book, in that it took the form of 'the eradication of inherited psychic structures', or habits of thought. Secondly, Jameson says, in its more modernist iteration by Henry James or Dostoyevsky, realism turned towards innovative methods for the 'renewal of perception', which he calls 'defamiliarisation'. The realist authors of the latter part of the nineteenth century developed new techniques in conversation with the science and technology of their day to defamiliarise what appeared to be evident, inviting its audience to look again, or look deeper and differently at social phenomena in particular. The glitch is also a defamiliarisation device since it presents our relation to media in amplified or unconventional settings, making the 'known' and habitual aspects of media unfamiliar again. What is interesting for a glitch poetics reading is how demystification and defamiliarisation operate in the literature of an age that is replete with oscillations between mystification/demystification and familiarity/

defamiliarisation, which is how code operations and media updates work (and fail).

The question that arises is: what is the role for realism when the world is simultaneously manifestly available – even the most base, uncommon and banal behaviours offered their few moments of fame on social media, and our own intimacies leaking out into corporate data sets and dark-web markets – while our everyday experience appears so manifestly strange, seen as it is through the 'black mirror' of technology as it oscillates between high fidelity and hyper-filtered representational modes?

Realism and Expanded Views

Søren Pold (2000) has shown that Balzac's rendering of nineteenth-century Paris as a literary image was inspired by a defamiliarising view offered by his day's newest visual mass medium technology. For Pold, significant moments in Balzac's novels are not only mounted, as with Baudelaire, on the dissociative 'atmosphere' of Paris during this era but are also informed by large scale 'panoramic' art installations that were popular at the time. The panorama was a social spectacle first patented by the Scottish painter, engineer and inventor Robert Barker in 1787. It involved displaying the city on a 360-degree canvas within a specific technical apparatus where viewers were offered successive views on a landscape (usually of a city), at different viewing platforms placed at varying heights at the centre of the image (fig. 15).

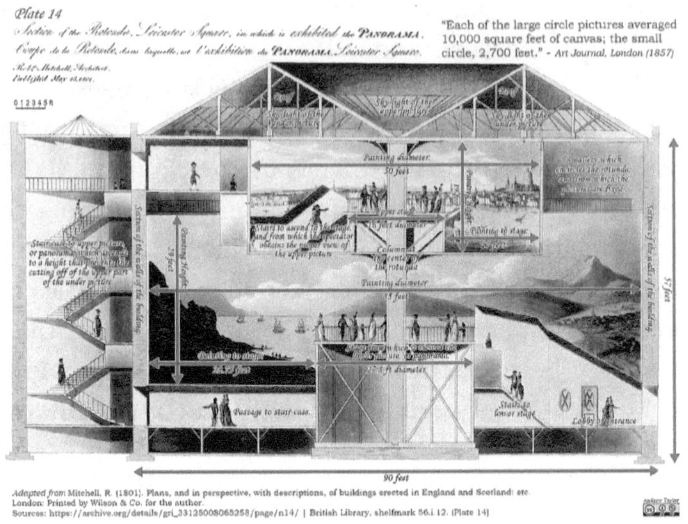

Fig. 15. Robert Mitchell's drawings for a rotunda, 1801. The rotunda was designed and built by Mitchell for Robert Barker, inventor of the painted panorama. This adaptation incorporates the architect's own description and key into the diagram. Andrew Taylor CC BY-SA 4.0.

The panoramic image disrupted Balzac's understanding of the demands for representation in the modern age. For Pold, 'the overall view of the city [was] mediated through the panorama' in Balzac's subsequent work (2000, 53). In the synthetic three-hundred-and-sixty degree view, he saw a mandate for a new kind of authorial technique. Specifically, Balzac's understanding that field of view could be expanded beyond the individual to encapsulate the entire city informed his use of the omniscient narrative voice and placed it in tension with the strange alienation of his characters. Previously unthinkable contradictions were generated in the mind of the author and their literary protagonists by the defamiliarising encounter with the city in the form of the panorama. As Pold says, Jules, the protagonist of Balzac's *Ferragus*, 'acknowledges with resignation that a total view of the city is larger than his field of vision' (52).

The evolving picture of reality afforded to literature today is ever more entangled in the question of omniscience raised by Balzac and other authors during the nineteenth century. What is fascinating for the question of literary realism is the degree to which the omniscient mode adopted by Balzac can be seen today–perhaps glitched through the defamiliarising lens of the modernist and postmodern novel – in the form of the rapaciously high-resolution digital subjects modelled at planetary scale. We now live in a world that has been built around anticipated behaviours of our imagined others. What forms of realism, fictional or otherwise, can help to articulate that? Can there be literature that answers the technical demands of a moment? As Geoff Cox and Mitra Azar ask in a recent essay: '[H]ow is the world made knowable to us when much of its operations lay outside our visual register and consequently outside the scope of human action?' (2021).

These questions are addressed in *Presense* (Gorlatova et al. 2020), a fictional digital platform designed by participants in the New Normal programme at the Strelka Institute in Moscow. *Presence* allows 'for the creation and tracking of personal synthetic replicas navigating multiple urban environments in parallel'. It is a (fictional, but proposed) piece of software that enables users to see what various versions of themselves, as 'personalised predictive models ... trained from user interaction', might be doing at any given moment. Using the software, the artists suggest, we would be able to watch automatically-generated Instagram posts, mapping data and financial records derived from our own phone use, but placed into virtual situations in various actual cites. Somehow, dormant in the expansive literary voice of Balzac, the vast panorama of the city has exploded to become a multi-city viewpoint, in which we are conceivably distributed across the globe in the form of virtual versions of ourselves. Authored by machines, we are living out possible futures and acting in strange ways in an unknowably complex cloud. This notional platform for iterating multiple actual actors from predictive text and big data 'refracted' from a single individual (an accelerated version of Scourti's [2015] work with predictive text technology) reminds us that the contemporary city is populated by digital imaginaries in which computers anticipate our 'real lives' in order to better orient us towards capital, and to better understand our digital representation's relationship to the reality we live in.

Digital Subject

As Goriunova (2018) says, the digital subject is the product of the alignment of different data types that we produce, consciously and unconsciously, with and without our permission and knowledge, by networked computational technologies. The digital subject that is created through the alignment of data can take the form of high-resolution documentation of a particular individual (their movements mapped through GPS, their tastes and preferences inferred from web-searches, clicks and memberships, their job roles, health outlook and social surroundings derived from image sets composited over many years). Equally, it can be a ghost without a shell, an imaginary of the system produced through inference only. Goriunova characterises the digital subject as a 'distance' between the data-sphere's ongoing production of representations of the subjects required for its functioning and the real-world individuals fleetingly remapped or twisted to fit their digital representations. Any given digital subject does not necessarily exist at all: what 'I' is flickers in and out of existence in this crowded, haunted fiction of digital subjectivity.

The fictional, networked nature of subjectivity in the digital also means that a particular digital subject is not necessarily indexed to a specific 'real world' individual, but rather is an imaginary of data-analysis that the system seeks to remap onto the world. These remappings are sites where the glitch happens as surprising encounters with slightly wrong versions of the self – or with uncannily real apparitions of inhuman data sets. For example, one healthy individual in Liverpool in the UK was recently surprised to be invited for a vaccine during the first weeks of the vaccination programme. On inquiry, he found out that the data held on him showed he was just 6.5cm tall and had a body mass index of 28,000. In another glitch event, a letter advertising baby products was 'mistakenly' posted out by the retailer Target to a Minneapolis high school student. The father receiving the letter on behalf of his daughter complained, understandably upset that the retailer appeared to be coercing his daughter into getting pregnant. The letter was sent by an automated service because the girl was exhibiting early pregnancy's behavioural tropes. Though neither the father nor his daughter knew at the time, the algorithm was correct; she *was* pregnant. When it is wrong and when it is accurate, our encounter with the digital subject floating in the system – as a gap between our understanding of what is real – presents to us as glitches between the imaginary of networked computers and the world we know.

The digital subject imagined by the network is analogous to the image of reality produced in the space between actually lived events and the fictional realisms of our day. Since its emergence, realism has been a dominant cultural force in delineating what we understand about ourselves. The question of who we are and how we really feel, and this question's entanglement with the fact-fiction distance of the digital subject, is addressed in the genre of auto-fiction. As Goriunova points out, in the context of data-prediction algorithms, 'the logic of fact arranged by data science carries some forms of fiction', and 'the logic of fiction [that we see in art today]... calls upon the logics of fact' (Goriunova 2018, 140) – that is, it engages with the apparent facticity of technically recorded forms of reality. Pushing this idea further in their book *Fictioning*, O'Sullivan and Burrows note that it is precisely what is not-real – that is, what is fictional – in literature, that constitutes its generative dimension and its contribution to science: what they call the 'mytho-poetic' function of art, which 'diagrams' new space for reality to move into (Burrows and O'Sullivan 2019, 13). Science fiction and 'speculative' art practices fall into this category, but so might contemporary fiction that purports to translate latent aspects of the media sphere into a style. Some authors, like digital artists, fictionalise the *emergent* qualities of a time as lived at the cutting edge of labour and social tension, using figural speech, for example (as in the case of Hito Steyerl [2015], who talks of virtual 3D protestors joining real-world marches, or Jennet Thomas, whose *Unspeakable Freedom Device* I analyse later in this chapter), to draw attention to an immanent form of reality. Autofiction authors emphasise the emergent ideas of data malleability to produce narrative 'errors' as deviations from established modes of realism. The characters in these books seem to flicker in and out of existence like flocks of data points.

Internet Realism Autofiction Glitch

So far, I have shown that realism is a genre with a double life: one foot in the gritty cut-and-thrust of the present rendered using habits inherited from the literature that 'works' for us, and another in the speculative territories of a techno-linguistic future, experienced as 'weirdness' or irreality, fault-lines in what literature should be. Contemporary autofiction (autobiography-fiction) straddles this divide, aiming to combine a truthful rendering of today's social conditions with strange narratological events and 'fictionings' that speculate on the embodied conditions of our ever-closer relationship with creepy new media. A particular recent strain of authors from the US, such as Tao Lin, Ben Lerner, Sheila Heti and Lauren Oyler, and Sally Rooney from Ireland, render pre-social, emergent forms of consciousness in their own manifestly odd literary approaches. These appear to be the product of a concerted stylistic attempt to occupy the space of the digital subject. However, as I have already suggested, the floaty 'atmosphere' of the internet portrayed in these books is not necessarily the one that is operative lower down the social strata.

'Internet age' autofiction authors develop on modern and postmodern realism by specifically distorting – or glitching, by holding at the indeterminate relationship between – the self with its fictionalised form. What is fascinating is the textural similarity between the glitches of digital imagery and the kinds of literary images favoured by auto-fiction authors. In many of these works, such as Rooney's *Conversations with Friends,* which the *New Yorker* described as a 'new kind of adultery novel' (Schwartz 2017), there is a trope where characters lose their definition and dissolve into the background: 'At this point I felt a weird lack of self-recognition, and I realised that I couldn't visualise my own face or body at all. It was like someone had lifted the end of an invisible pencil and just gently erased my entire appearance. This was curious and actually not unpleasant, though I was also aware that I was cold and might have been shivering' (Rooney 2017, 87). In Tao Lin's novel *Taipei,* there is a similar phenomenon to Rooney's 'lack of self-recognition' where the fringes of the protagonist's sensorium glitch, dissolve and distribute themselves into the wider world: 'Paul ... felt continuously aroused "somewhere", including sometimes, it seemed, outside his body, a few feet in front of him, or far in the distance, in a certain store or area of sky, or in an overlap, shifting in and out of his chest or head or the front of his face' (Lin 2012, 435). The character's phenomenological experience appears to have been displaced by the distributed processes of the internet-enabled phone and laptop he habitually and obsessively views the world through throughout the novel. Indeed, Lin's unsettlingly 'flat' prose, like the ubiquitous flat lighting of Taipei's superstores and malls in which the book is set, also seems to embody the distinctive affect-depleting quality of spending large amounts of time on social media. His sensoria are offset into the world in the same manner as his thoughts and utterances exist in 'the cloud' accessible through his devices.

In Megan Boyle's *LIVEBLOG* (2018) the dissolving boundaries trope is associated with a kind of dissociation from the author's own thoughts: 'something happened. looked like pictures were coming out of my phone. Red-orange lights on the edges of peripheral vision are twinkling mildly. Sometimes there is a blue light. Realised this via thinking "is it a cop moving towards me"' (Boyle 2018). This kind of dissociation is perhaps unsurprising, given the frequency with which the authors write through moments where they fall asleep in the light of their phones or laptops. Boyle (and also the female protagonist in Lin's *Taipei*) pushes this aspect of her work by writing through dissociative events, leaving the glitchy writing that results intact in the final manuscript.

> 12:22AM: bathwater is running. i'm just going ot do this until forever. ate half of some kind of pill, 1 mg Xanax ithink. ...
>
> ookkk anoth athter xaanxn at some e oo==ibe, ijay sruffl is going to better e=vetter i know
>
> (Boyle 2018)

The trope of dissolving boundaries as an echo of the embodiment of distinctive media devices can also be found in contemporaneous works by Patricia Lockwood:

> Her fingertips, her ears, her sleepiness and her wide awake, a ripple along the skin wherever she was touched. All along her edges, just where she turned to another state. (2021, 253)
>
> A fizzing black void opened behind her eyes, where the long backward root of her sight was. (2021, 151)

And even in Elena Ferrante's period work, the main character experiences breakdowns that to me rhyme with the internet novelists', in their dissolution of material into virtual forms:

> [S]he had often had the sensation of moving for a few fractions of a second into a person or a thing or a number or a syllable, violating its edges. And the day her father threw her out the window she had felt absolutely certain, as she was flying toward the asphalt, that small, very friendly reddish animals were dissolving the composition of the street, transforming it into a smooth, soft material. But that New Year's Eve she had perceived for the first time unknown entities that broke down the outline of the world and demonstrated its terrifying nature. (Ferrante 2012, 91)

The way these authors glitch their language and use glitches to relate their characters' internal lives does not necessarily link to any expert knowledge the authors have of the media ecology. In this way these literary glitches differ from the approach of authors such as Breeze, who deploy textures or tropes of the digital as a sign of their knowing involvement in the digital. Instead, the autofiction lossy-edges trope and its connection to error is an 'authentic' glitch in the colloquial sense of the term: a kind of shock effect taking place in the body as it responds to wrong inputs or overloads. These 'authentic' glitches also have a sort of prototypical edge; they are the 'structures of feeling' (Williams 1977) of an imminent mainstream sensation. As digital media become ever more integrated into our sensoria and cognitive processes, and we become more closely identified with digital subjects through our interactions with the network project, the lossy edges sensation will become more commonplace.

The inclusion of media conditions as a style in internet age autofiction displaces and adds latency to the kinds of lived reality articulated in previous autobiographical fictions. The internet age autofiction author reimagines a formal quality of digital media as a particular kind of unease within the production of the self. The media archaeology scholar Wolfgang Ernst would suggest that today's media *temporalise* experience in a way that resonates with the reports of the autofiction authors (Ernst 2017, 14). As I observed in the previous chapter, the exceptional quality of digital temporality of the kind Ernst writes about can be observed in early glitch work. In fact, Melissa Feldman's description of Murata's datamoshed videos, in which he digitally compresses video footage so it records only the net difference in movement from one frame to the next, almost sounds like an image from the internet novelist: 'Frustrating the gaze, her beautiful face never stays still long enough to really be looked at. Instead, it keeps distorting to monstrous proportions, turning into liquid reflections. ... Atmosphere and ambiguity prevail here' (Feldman, 2006). So one explanation would be that the dissolving boundaries phenomenon in Rooney and Lin accelerates the unease of a digital media image 'irritated by the present' by imagining it as an embodied condition. Indeed, in *Liveblog* Megan Boyle describes her mental pictures as 'a lot of fast-moving mental picture things. seems foreign ... it's like when the edges of 8-bit things become softer in .jpegs' (2018, 214).

Goriunova's notion of the digital subject allows us to observe that it is not just images and sounds that are subjected to micro-temporal adjustments and interferences. Instead, the big data computer network's imaginary of the crowd 'is constantly produced, re-instantiated, re-engendered, refreshed', in ways that imagine individuals not within stable bodies, but rather as 'values, dynamically re-instantiated correlations, rules, and models, shreds of actions, identities, interests, and engagements, which are put into relation with each other' (Goriunova 2018, 142). This evokes the protagonist's position in the internet age novel; a condition experienced through the authors' interface with word processors, email and social media is extrapolated for them into an ontology for their characters. In fact, Goriunova makes an analogy between the writing of digital subjects by computer networks and the author's work, noting that we have all inadvertently become authors as 'we write ourselves by generating data that is worked upon and then produced as digital subjects, which are inconsistent and not very coherent' (136).

What is also interesting is the pull Goriunova identifies in the network 'to map computed digital subjects onto human beings' (136), and how the dissolving boundaries trope in internet novels coincides with the auto-fiction genre in which authors appear to use their own lives as a malleable material for fictioning. Sometimes there is a meta-commentary on this in internet-age autofiction. At one point in *Taipei* Lin imagines that one of the incidental characters in the book has inadvertently imagined the main protagonists into being:

> a young man in Taipei, while eating a bag of Chicken McNuggets, [who] allowed himself...
> to realistically imagine his next binge, when he would have two bags
>
> ...
>
> Paul and Erin were constructed by the young man's unconscious, for verisimilitude, as passersby in the peripheral vision of his imaginary next trip to McDonalds. (Lin 2012)

Fiction and fact are blurred in this vignette in a way that is reflective of the current techno-capital condition, told by the narrators to each other, and narrated into the video-editing app on Paul's laptop as they wander around the city. Each of these characters is quite likely interpellated in the distance of the digital subject by commercial technology in the highly mediated environment of the Taipei mall, unwittingly playing the role of training and resourcing an increasingly high-resolution big-data image of typical McDonald's visitors. As with Rooney, Lockwood and Boyle, the method of fictioning the world through social media existing in mutable digital archives becomes an embodied condition.

At times, though, the embodiment of the informatic condition by characters in these books can seem like nothing more than the privileges of a particular set of author-journalists turned into a sense of being. Events in the novels frequently appear to be at the bidding of the central characters, without any of the material or pragmatic concerns we might typically expect. For authors such as Lauren Oyler, we live in a 'social media-addled world saturated with loneliness and alienation' (D'Aprile 2021), having real-world implications that seem perversely frictionless. This has some striking effects on the nature of the plot in these books. One of Oyler's central character's crises culminates like this: 'we cried and then I felt like I needed to leave the country, so here I was'. Similarly, in Ben Lerner's 2015 novel *10:04* (2015), there is a sense that the author is a kind of swipe-editing curator of reality, and this does not resonate with people from less well-heeled backgrounds. As well as the need to experiment in search of apposite defamiliarised renderings of its time, the realist genre can also focus on the experience of 'ordinary', and of 'working people' – particularly seeing as they are often the individuals who most intensely embody the characteristic stress and conflicts of their time. As I suggested at the beginning of the chapter, this immediately suggests a more disjunctive form of glitch.

Structures of Feeling

Glitch poetics connects the work of glitch ideas to the historical importance of realist literature in defining the scope of human and social sensoria in a way that evokes the literary 'affect theory' of Raymond Williams (1977). Williams suggests that discontinuities in literary style – departing from dominant trends – convey emergent and pre-emergent forms of the social-to-come as affective 'felt' qualities of attentive reading. By definition, pre-emergent attributes do not exist within fixed forms or genres, nor do they coalesce into new ones *yet*, but rather exhibit themselves as displacements or latencies, compared to the mainstream. This means that literature speculating on social transformations latent in today's reality is either errant or conspicuous in its absence.

Williams emphasises the difficulty of reading for what he calls the 'structures of feeling' that have a speculative character because they appear in the form of tensions with existing structures that are ill-defined or not immediately evident (perhaps because they are taken for granted) rather than meaningful in themselves: 'the tension is as often an unease, a stress, a displacement, a latency: the moment of conscious comparison not yet come, often not even coming' (1977: 183). Willliams' description evokes for me the tension between 'resignation' and 'stimulation' felt by Balzac's Jules in *Ferragus* on encountering the panorama, for example, a sense that a 'known unknown' has become apparent. It also certainly evokes the strange dissociative latencies between virtual and actual in the novels of the internet-age authors. Structures of feeling are the signs within texts of an 'ambiguous configuration of the social that has not yet fully emerged' but is present in personal consciousnesses – and in the emphatic present-ness of literature and art. For Williams,

> This process can be directly observed in the history of a language. In spite of substantial and at some levels decisive continuities in grammar and vocabulary, no generation speaks quite the same language as its predecessors. The difference can be defined in terms of additions, deletions, and modifications, but these do not exhaust it. What really changes is something quite general, over a wide range, and the description that often fits the change best is the literary term 'style'. (Williams 1977: 187)

In Williams' essay on the Welsh industrial novel (Williams 2010: 47-52), he specifies an example of the displacements and stresses that constitute a structure of feeling concerning the particular conditions of Welsh mining communities during the early 20th century.

Williams proceeds with his analysis firstly by comparison with English industrial fiction. The Welsh industrial novel arrives much later than its English counterpart, and it is in this sense 'a latency ... a conspicuous comparison not yet come'. When it does arrive, the Welsh industrial novel reflects the distinctive tensions and displacements of industrialisation as they are felt by the Welsh: the confined gritty work of the underground mine is different from the collective, mechanically-temporalised labours of the factory. Williams finds this social distinction in the rendering of landscape and the forms of family relations plotted in the Welsh novels. Williams' analysis in this mode is elliptical and tendentious, in that it rarely settles on specific details or examples. Instead, he writes along perceived lines of commonality between various Welsh novels as they parallel their English counterparts, 'feeling' for the 'deepest basic movement of all this writing' (2010, 223). In effect, he attempts to read across the distance between the particulars and details in Welsh industrial novels and the idea of the Welsh novel as a body of work, looking for the distinctive nature of the Welsh individual and social body in this historical period. He suggests that the social consciousness's emerging 'hopes and possibilities' at this particular turning point in Welsh history can be detected as a shape, 'the slope, the skyline to be seen immediately from the streets and from the pit-tops', and in the 'contrasts of darkness and light, of being trapped and of getting clear' (223), articulated repeatedly in the Welsh novels of this era.

Additionally, Williams notes that generational narratives are articulated differently in realist Welsh literature of this time. The population are forced to travel abroad for work and learning. As a result, a fragmented, episodic, genre-blurring generational fiction emerges: 'industrial depression unites [the family] in a common condition and then pulls it this way and that, dividing or even breaking it, in the struggle for survival' (224):

> [T]he family is being pulled in one direction after another and yet that the family persists, but persists in a sense of defeat and loss. The bitter experience of that period – of the massive

> emigrations to England and yet of the intense and persistent family feeling of those who stay and those who remember – are then powerfully but always temporarily articulated: the moment of a very local sadness. (224)

The Welsh industrial novel departed from the English industrial novel partly because the family portrayed in each was different: perhaps most notably in the figure of the 'house', which in the English is haunted by previous generations, or untold secrets about the present, whereas in the Welsh it is pummelled, broken and 'persists' under external pressures. This difference contains within it the grain of an emergent social pattern. The 'slope' and 'contrasts of light and dark... of being trapped and getting clear' that are particular to the Welsh novel's rendering of the miners' experiences are also different from the 'desolate moors', 'pea-souper fogs' and 'family closets' that are the signature motifs of the English mainstream determined by writers such as Jane Austin and George Elliot during this period (Watt 1957).

In this sense, the shape and structure of the Welsh industrial novel anticipate the emergence of wholly distinctive Welsh realism in the modern day, such as Niall Griffiths' novel *Wreckage* (2005), which portrays the Welsh diaspora in Liverpool jammed into what Stevie Davies characterises as a 'bardic and apocalyptic' voice, and whose title evokes the kind of familial relations it relates. Indeed, as a Welsh man in the twenty-first century, I can well recognise the forms of displacement

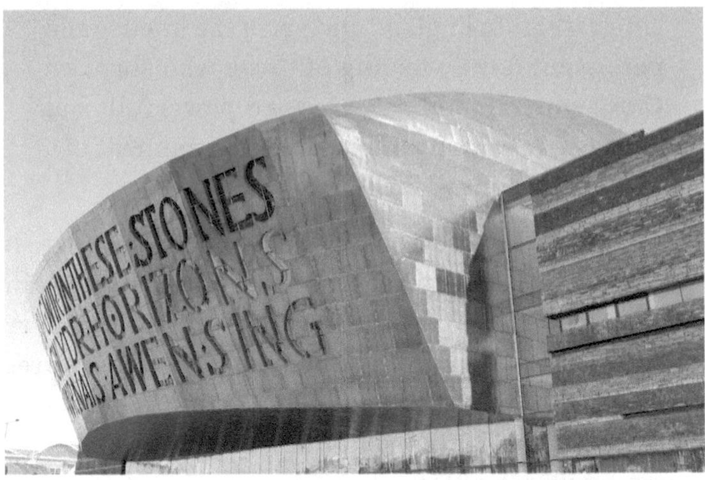

Fig. 16. Gordon Plant's Millennium Centre, Cardiff Bay, 2010, author's photo.

Williams divines in the literature of the nineteenth century as part of our national identity now. The country itself is fragmented across multiple lines: urban-rural, coastal-inland, north-south and English-Welsh speaking parts of the country exist in mutual alienation from one another. Many families are priced out of buying homes in the country's most attractive areas by people relocating from southern England and so live distant from their extended family. The signature development of Cardiff's dock front regeneration, the Millennium Stadium (fig. 16), carves a slope in the skyline that moved the poet Gwyneth Lewis to evoke the country's mining and horizons. On the frontage of the stadium, her commission reads, 'In these stones horizons sing'.

The Welsh industrial novel's latency was firstly expressed by its slow arrival. When it arrived, the cumulative effects of working life and landscape, before being internalised as a national identity, meant that it was very 'un-novelistic' compared to the field established during the English Industrial Era. The first 'structures of feeling' of the novels of the digital industry similarly may be slow to arrive due to the vicissitudes of living and publishing today.

Class, Realism and Language-Unease

As with environmental collapse, the excesses and instabilities of the emergent techno-sphere are not distributed evenly. Working-class people are more likely to experience the effects of technological 'advances' returning to them as unpredictable and unknowable commands on the mind and body. By this logic, we could observe, the poor and other marginalised groups experience and speak of the future first,[27] but in ways that appear wrong or ill-suited to their time and that are slow or difficult to recognise in their literary form.

The current generations of low-wage labour internationally are subjected in unique ways by the digital. To select one aspect of the kind of worker whose labour undergirds the internet economy, the Uber driver is formed at the intersection of GPS, user-interfaces, user behaviour, voice-assisted navigation, locally applied demand economics, international time differentials and the global corporate culture. Uber drivers will not write their characters dissolving or appearing and disappearing at will, as I have observed of the 'internet novelists', but rather feel that movement, and a kind of ever-present alertness, as the signature characteristic of life. At the same time, their cognitive experience, rather than floaty and jpg-like, may be characterised by flows of intensity, bursts of silence, part-stories that blend into a high-definition impressionistic rendering of the city, physical threat, sleeplessness, urgency and a demand more akin to that of on-demand streaming services.

There are books written from this perspective by Uber drivers, consciously drawn from their particular view on the city and relations with it, such as the crime genre work of Adrian McKinty (2019). There is a different texture in McKinty's novels. For example, numbness is not associated with the stillness and torpidity it might have in 'internet-age' work, but rather with a continually unstoppable motion: 'The numbness. The feeling of plunging into the abyss and falling, falling, falling forever' (McKinty 2019, 97). The plot of McKinty's *The Chain* is also radically different to the louche mode of autofiction narrative. It involves its characters being locked into seemingly irresolvable obligations to which they are held by seemingly omniscient antagonists.

However, while the language of a generation of journalists and editors who are associated with digital subjectivity in the form of the internet novel seems like it has been collectively honed through online dialogues, Uber drivers, like other members of the digital precariat, are denied places to congregate, let alone publish and share work together. The novels from individuals such as McKinty, while containing interesting tensions that may connect to the unique way their bodies have been exposed to digital contexts, are currently formally generic, without the confidence or publishing infrastructure to nurture a language of alterity. A shared literature of the digital precariat will be slow to emerge, and a sense of 'the structure of feeling' of these works is difficult to analyse from such a sparse field. There is a latency here that is itself a point of analysis. In the next section, I want to look at the possibilities for contemporary working-class language error through the lens of 'social vernaculars' and then think about how these kinds of error may be rendered as literary styles.

Vernacular as Error

People speak a social vernacular based on their own 'lifeworld': a kind of composite of languages adopted from the various spheres they operate in as everyday people. We can think of this vernacular as analogous to the 'interaction gestalt' formed by our habitual uses of new media devices (Menkman 2010). Like media, the default vernacular is a way of interfacing with the world; it has been formed by combinations of technical and social disruption and habituation (Chun 2016).

There are various interrelated languages that we use to operate in different lifeworlds, which in turn interpellate us a position, called 'social vernaculars' (Gee 2017). Most people adopt a more formal version of their own social vernacular to show deference to elders or to acknowledge a lack of common ground between the speaker and their audience. However, working-class people are less likely to switch vernacular in their day-to-day life. This can be for various reasons: working-class people are less likely and less well prepared than middle-class people to encounter and transact with those outside of the working-class lifeworld, and so are less fluent in formal vernacular; or they are less deferential to authority, more suspicious of what is to be lost in their switching of vernaculars; or they are simply less likely to understand the function of switching. The result is that working-class people more often adopt the 'wrong' combination of the formal and informal vernaculars for any given situation, and therefore find themselves speaking *and feeling* out of place; or (and this is more common in its literary form) they adopt the default formal vernacular too readily and in an unnaturally blended way.

It is against this default for the social vernacular that specific lifeworld languages – whether specialist jargons or informal vernacular uses of dialect – are read culturally as insubordinate displays of aggressive impropriety, 'experimental' style or obtuse difficulty. The dominance of the middle-class in British literature, in particular, means that the formal version of everyday language has also become a default style of literary address. And so, integrating un-switched or improperly switched language into literature often means it will be harder to publish, an overlap between the literary and social forms of language that reify the middle class's over-representation in the literary field (Lock 2021). It has been noted that the specifically British sense of class and vernacular propriety may have shaped the kinds of radicalism and resistance found in our poetics. Peter Middleton describes this as a significant difference between American and British language-focused poetry:

> [A US] poet such as William Carlos Williams was inclined 'to see and treat language as an object in itself', while modern British counterparts have not been able to do this so readily because of the degree to which language is thought of in terms of proper and improper usage. The ability to use standard English is a marker of education and social status, and because 'correct' voice or pronunciation is such a social value, the force field of correctness distorts all perceptions of language. (Middleton 2015, 18)

Middleton suggests that the American inheritors of 'objectivists' such as Williams have combined a tendency to 'see and treat language as an object' (17). For them, post-structuralist theory constitutes a poetic mandate in which poem-objects should be able to force readers to reconsider their position concerning language through forms of disjunction, such as parataxis. In contrast, the typical British avant-gardist tends to depict reader-writer interactions as contaminated by language's role in social, fiscal and industrial systems, distorting and corrupting it in advance. British avant-garde writers typically are more aware that in speaking (and writing), they are marked within their social strata.

In 'Wot We Wokkers Wunt' (1980), Steve McCaffery kludges *The Communist Manifesto* through Yorkshire dialect: so the opening reads 'na see thee there's a boogie mr bothering all o'r uh place and its boogie mr uh-communism... all gaffers in all Europe got all Churchified to bush it aaht' (my transcription). And the lines from Marx and Engels' manifesto that read: 'our epoch, the epoch of the bourgeoisie, possesses, however, this distinct feature: it has simplified class antagonisms. Society as a whole is more and more splitting up into two great hostile camps, into two great classes directly facing each other – Bourgeoisie and Proletariat' (Marx and Engels 1848) is rendered by McCaffery as 'We still got these kind of bashups I mean thumpers a different, but thump-up's just about the same. But nowaways we got onto something a bit different and it's this: we bloody well know who we're bashing. It's them that's gaffers and us that isn't' (McCaffery 1980). The effect here is of a corruption and distortion of the existing text that at once distances it from the original, making the language less 'clear', while simultaneously clarifying the message within the infamous document, defamiliarising it and pushing it against a working person's vocabulary.

Similarly, British Caribbean poets such as Derek Walcott and Linton Kwesi Johnson purposefully jam 'proper' literary vernacular with the creole language: a form of dialect that is frequently considered as a mistaken form of speech but is actually a language system with syntaxes and grammars, resulting from colonial activity in the Caribbean, though these are not standardised in the way they are used (Donellson and Welsh 1996, 8). As Walcott says, creole language exists in 'defiance of an imperial concept of language', and he finds outside of this imperial language a 'freshness' that echoes the language of poetry: 'this process of renaming, of finding new metaphors, is the same. process that the poet faces every morning of his working day, making his own tools' (in Donnellson and Welsh 1996, 403). Vernaculars and dialects are often encountered as corruptions and errors in literary language, and, like error, they can bring a new critical potential to the material of literature by taking it outside of pre-programmed linguistic habits and emphasising the textural quality of what has caused the 'error'.

The sense that reader-writer interactions are contaminated by colonial and class structures is echoed in the post-digital conceit: the digital, like coloniality, compromises our ability to write but is impossible to write outside of because it forms the basis of the infrastructures we write through and with. Some performance writers look to older and emphatically material modes of writing that predate the digital, their use of non-computational media 'calling into question the common assumption that computers, as meta-machines, represent obvious technological progress and therefore constitute a logical upgrade from any older media technology' (Cramer 2015). Post-digital practice, like post-colonial writing, seeks to historicise its context, framing the digital as something that has already happened and can be disrupted. The performance writing practitioner Roy Claire Potter does this effectively in *Mental Furniture*. This book was composed on a 'sticky' typewriter and is published as a first draft so that troubles with accent, speech and the spelling of a working-class vernacular are combined with typing errors: 'Mother not me mum. Me-mum in speech because me-mumse Moy Mother. Not 'Me mum Mother, not me-mum. In speech: me-mum. Not here. Mother. Motherhood' (Potter 2014, 10). Slips with the typewriter, lines that are rethought 'live' by Potter and slang and vernacular terms such as 'me mum' that are not mistakes but nevertheless register as 'non-literary' are pushed into combination with one another in this text. By this gesture, Potter connects the struggle with the typewriter, the unforgiving nature of its analogue interface and the lack of autocorrect functions with other aspects of what is challenging about writing: the act of recall, its articulation into words and the rendering of those words by the body, the polished surface of fluency. As they reflect in an interview with their publisher that accompanies the book, 'Maybe all these techniques are what in another sort of book would be description and character. It's interesting to imagine someone picking up the book and complaining about typos and other mistakes because that would be to deny any sense that spelling and grammar are mutable to the rhythms of our bodyminds' (Potter 2014).

In the case of Potter, the typewriter's stickiness and the way it records human erring, errors, hesitations and reworkings are made to stand in for the body-minds susceptibility to other forms of injury and struggle: Potter frequently evokes the harm caused to the subconscious by traumatic events, for example, and their own working-class background, with its unique proximities and domestic tensions. As we read *Mental Furniture,* the repetitions and hesitations in the text are 'played back' like tremors of traumatic events in the body and an analogy is made between working-class language, the work of writing and the material and emotional pressures of the domestic scene.

Proto-Media-Realisms of Modernism

Writing today's workplace requires recuperating unconventional linguistic and formal choices that were the signature quality of modernist literature from the line of bourgeois linguistic innovation and 'difficulty' that has come since, and plugging them back into the egalitarian aspects of the realist project in ways demonstrated by artists such as Potter. There is a rich vein of working-class experimental British literature from the post-war period, recently traced by Andrew Hodgson. However, whereas Hodgson emphasises the effects of the World Wars on the novel, resulting in tropes of 'silence, amnesia, psychological wounds, or a persisting nightmare' (2019, 22), the contemporary traumata that I am interested in with relation to the digital subject have to do with modes of interpellation, compulsion and automation that come from digital subjectivity and precarity.

There is a latency between the experimental post-war novel and the experience of workers in today's media climates, which can be identified by the absence of errors of a certain kind in contemporary work. Nevertheless, we can find the contemporary worker's technical situation anticipated in proto-realist works from an earlier age, which project (or fiction) the future worker in their glitch textures and errant forms. What I would like to do now is revisit two canonical experimental works from the start of the 'information revolution' and 'globalisation' as examples where the 'structures of feeling' of these then-nascent cultures were being written. In them, I suggest, we can discern the structures of feeling of current conditions for people in today's workplaces.

Language as Information in *Watt*

Samuel Beckett was one of the first authors to encounter code in its early human-machine iterations, catching and promulgating the viral quality of encoded text in his early novel *Watt*. Laura Salisbury has noted that the permutational quality of *Watt*, written during the Second World War, should be understood through the lens of his participation in the GLORIA SMH spy network in occupied France. In particular, Salisbury focuses on Beckett's role in processing, collating and translating secret messages. She quotes from Beckett's diaries: 'I would type it all out clean. Put it in order and type it out, on one sheet of paper, as far as was possible ... My sheets would be reduced to the size of a matchbox.

All the information. Probably unreadable but it could be magnified' (in Salisbury 2014, 156). Salisbury's use of this biographical detail lends great weight to the theory that Beckett's work was a response to latent qualities of the information processes embedded in war-time communication. As she comments:

> Language at this historical moment demands to be understood within a more general but more complex paradigm of information. Language is plastic enough to be broken down into bits, the information it carries to be condensed and displaced or submitted to encryption, and then transmitted under technical conditions which, though they may preserve the signal to a degree, understand it always to be fighting what thermodynamics had shown to be a fundamentally losing battle against the noise immanent within any of channel communication. (156)

Watt's overly literal, logical thought processes are a kind of error (perhaps today we would recognise this character as being autistic [Michaud 2017]), and they ironically put him at odds with a world that contains illogical errors that he cannot absorb. For example, Watt spends much of the novel ruminating how a door could have been found to be open after he had already checked it and found it to be closed. There is a manner to this contradiction of language and world that anticipates the oscillating glitch ontologies of running code. This sequence where Watt attempts to name and identify something evokes a kind of machine learning apparatus stuck in a logic loop:

> Looking at a pot, for example, or thinking of a pot, at one of Mr Knott's pots, of one of Mr Knott's pots, it was in vain that Watt said, Pot, pot. Well, perhaps not quite in vain, but very nearly. For it was not a pot, the more he looked, the more he reflected, the more he felt sure of that, that it was not a pot at all. It resembled a pot, it was almost a pot, but it was not a pot of which one could say, Pot, pot, and be comforted. It was in vain that it answered, with unexceptionable adequacy, all the purposes, and performed all the offices, of a pot, it was not a pot. And it was just this hair-breadth departure from the nature of a true pot that so excruciated Watt. For if the approximation had been less close, then Watt would have been less anguished. For then he would not have said, This is a pot, and yet not a pot, no, but then he would have said, This is something of which I do not know the name. And... (Beckett 1953, 67)

Formally, the novel is constituted of sequences of overlapping compulsive sentences of this kind driven by a permutational approach to syntax, which transition into each other or are interrupted and restart. The narrative involves its protagonist sliding into madness via an obsessive and exacting logic, as they accumulate ever longer and more arduous language operation confinements.

The compulsive, machinic quality of *Watt* is neatly reflected in Nick Montfort's *Megawatt*: 'a novel computationally, deterministically generated extending passages from Samuel Beckett's *Watt*' (2014, 3), which features passages written by a machine using English-language syntax as a generative engine, which end up looking remarkably like the human-written passages in the original:

> And the poor old lousy earth, my earth and my father's and my mother's and my father's father's and my father's mother's and my mother's father's and my mother's mother's and my father's father's father's and my father's father's mother's and my father's mother's father's and my father's mother's mother's and my mother's father's father's and my mother's father's mother's and my mother's mother's father's and my mother's mother's mother's and my father's father's father's father's and my father's father's father's mother's and my father's father's mother's father's and my father's father's mother's mother's and my father's mother's father's father's and my father's mother's father's mother's. (Montfort 2014, 14)

Montfort's work doesn't simply point to an affinity between Beckett's WWII-era novel and the generative literature of today, but instead makes an observation about the astuteness of Beckett's emphasis on generative grammars, about how much sense it makes of the conditions for computing that were embedded in the code work he was then involved in. *Watt* contained an unease that gestured towards an emergent shift in language: language as information would come to imply humans as data processes, simultaneously informed and comparatively unsure of themselves.

Evoking the figure of the Uber driver, one recent critic likens Watt's mode of consciousness to 'a G.P.S. that continues to recalculate routes long after the driver has abandoned the original destination' (Michaud 2017). There is a sense that the main character is being subjected to this errant mode of thinking by an out-of-control language. In this same mode, James Bridle's article, 'Something is Wrong on the Internet', documents a new breed of digital worker who is driven to make a particular kind of content to feed YouTube's 'next up' algorithm. The result is a genre of creepy video in which people perform short, repetitive, 'zany' actions with slight variations for long periods, in ways that stimulate and placate very young children who are left in front of the screen. The makers of these videos, Bridle observes, are trapped, 'endlessly acting out the implications of a combination of algorithmically generated keywords' with titles such as

> Halloween Finger Family & more Halloween Songs for Children | Kids Halloween Songs Collection', 'Australian Animals Finger Family Song | Finger Family Nursery Rhymes', 'Farm Animals Finger Family and more Animals Songs | Finger Family Collection - Learn Animals Sounds', 'Safari Animals Finger Family Song |

> Elephant, Lion, Giraffe, Zebra & Hippo! Wild Animals for kids', 'Superheroes Finger Family and more Finger Family Songs! Superhero Finger Family Collection', 'Batman Finger Family Song – Superheroes and Villains! Batman, Joker, Riddler, Catwoman' and on and on and on. (Bridle 2014)

As Bridle observes, 'this is content production in the age of algorithmic discovery – even if you're a human, you have to end up impersonating the machine'. The maddening and hypnotically repetitious loops of Watt's behaviour anticipate this mode of labour, where computers' latent biases produce demand for 'wrong' human performance as labour. This is an extreme example of a generalised condition for work in a world where value is calculated according to essentially unknowable machine logics. *Watt* provides a view of the innards of the language structures inside the computational and networked technologies that our own actions are thoroughly entangled with today.

The prose of *Watt* is also simultaneously maddening and comforting, zany and placating, in a way that resonates with the internet ephemera Bridle writes about, reminding us of the proximity of disruption and habit in the digital and literary world alike. Beckett has reportedly said that writing *Watt* 'kept him sane' during the World War II period. When I read *Watt* now, in the light of the ease with which Montfort's work will have been generated and thinking about the relationship between GPS and YouTube algorithms and their human performers, I am also struck by the presence of Beckett himself in *Watt*, in particular by how the trance-like experience of reading it reflects the repetitiousness of his writing process. In composing *Watt*, Beckett embodied a language machine, his body locked into thought-like habit-sentences, disrupted by bursts of feeling:

> And he wondered what the artist had intended to represent (Watt knew nothing about painting), a circle and its centre in search of each other, or a circle and its centre in search of a centre and a circle respectively, or a circle and its centre in search of its centre and a circle respectively, or a circle and its centre in search of a centre and its circle respectively, or a circle and a centre not its centre in search of its centre and its circle respectively, or a circle and a centre not its centre in search of a centre and a circle respectively, or a circle and a centre not its centre in search of its centre and a circle respectively, or a circle and a centre not its centre in search of a centre and its circle respectively, in boundless space, in endless time (Watt knew nothing about physics), and at the thought that it was perhaps this, a circle and a centre not its centre in search of a centre and its circle respectively, in boundless space, in endless time, then Watt's eyes filled with tears that he could not stem, and they flowed down his fluted cheeks unchecked, in a steady flow, refreshing him greatly. (Beckett 1953, 110)

In today's working-class experiences, digital instructions operate as a kind of relief from certain types of labour (finding an address, taking instructions from a taxi operator), replacing them with paradoxically relieving and demanding forms of automation that execute within the body of the labourer, perhaps resulting in maddening but at least 'easy' behaviours that are anticipated in Watt's characterisation. In this way, the notion of proto-realism provides a conceit for rereading the glitches of literature of previous eras – which perhaps seemed simply 'absurd' at the time – as reflecting something new about our current condition: one that is undoubtedly more disjunctive than is portrayed by the internet novelists, but that nonetheless may contain some clue as to why we so readily integrate it into our lives.

The Creole of The Wake

Another author attributed with having diagrammed new technical territory for language in their literary work is James Joyce. Though Joyce's *Ulysses* (1922) is more often read as a kind of extreme realist novel, his later *Finnegan's Wake* (1939) can also be read as realist in the light of emergent media and postcolonial conditions. As Jacques Derrida has noted, Joyce's language in *Finnegan's Wake* embodies the most intensively radical aspects of the 'grammatology' of technics, 'utilising a language that could equalise the greatest possible synchronicity with the greatest potential for buried, accumulated, and interwoven intentions within each linguistic atom, each vocable, each word, each simple proposition' (Derrida, quoted in Gere 2016, 13). Indeed, it is fascinating to observe now how glitchy – that is, *wrong-feeling* in a digital-seeming way – *Finnegan's Wake* reads to the contemporary reader:

> The prouts who will invent a writing there ultimately is the poeta, still more learned, who discovered the raiding there originally. That's the point of eschatology our book of kills reaches for now in soandso many counterpoint words. What can't be coded can be decorded if an ear aye sieze what no eye ere grieved for. Now, the doctrine obtains, we have occasioning cause causing effects and affects occasionally recawing altereffects. Or I will let me take it upon myself to suggest to twist the penman's tale posterwise. (Joyce 2012, 482)

An instructive comparison can certainly be made between Joyce's use of the neologism as a node of corruption and difficulty, and the work of Mez Breeze:

> pin.point.data.crow[s eye]ing (2005-04-01 05:13)
>
> slush.p[acket]uppied.+watching.golden.crow.
> eye .morphings.
>
> stagger.flite+anxiety.information.stringing.thru.a
>
> ndrenals+butter.cusp.back
>
> –ebony.swagger.fixtures+audio.[w(h)ip.e]crac
>
> kling.+.dragging.my.VOIPer.feat
>
> (Breeze 2012, 34)

These potentials and conflicts in more recent technologies can be seen in the visual poetry of Allison Parrish, who deploys the manner that AI autoencoders translate language corpora into statistical weightings to coin new hybrid terms at the average point between existing words' sounds and meanings in *Compass* (2020).

In my work with Tom Schofield and Sam Skinner, such as *Crash Blossoms* (2020), we deploy recursive neural nets to produce unwieldy hybrid language at the statistical intersection between different historical and contemporary headlines, articulating a difficult possibility for rendering the future from the remains of the past. In this case, as with Parrish's work, the computer can misspell in an apposite manner that provides the texture and potency of the work. Similarly, with Joyce, his hybrids are not unreadable, but in their manifest wrongness require a reassessment of the role of the non-representational aspects of language: the atomic-scale inference, assonance and relation-collisions that happen when we read and speak in a world where radically different forms of language are sampled at the character-level, making diverse 'live' vernaculars that rub up against our sluggish habits of reading. The affinities between this work, Parrish's, Breeze's and Joyce's, are numerous. They each use recombinant methods, breaking language from diverse sources and vernacular sets into phonemes and rearranging them according to unknowable logics, and, in so doing, extending the inference, physical and musical quality of words to expand the realm of the sayable. In part this affinity suggests that Joyce's engagement with film and the new sound recording technologies of the 1920s[28] led him to anticipate a vernacular generated by resampling existing global languages in the digital age.

A complementary reading of the strange spellings and assonances of *Finnegan's Wake* is that they were produced by the colonial context. In this case, Joyce's language can be shown to have affinities to the creole of Walcott, for example. The language in the *Wake* is thus what Homi Bhabha (2012) calls a 'language of cultural nonsense': an ambiguous hybrid that emerges in the context of cultural mixing under pressurised conditions, including unassimilable habits of speech, subterfuge in the face of oppression and a kind of internalised alienhood. Taking this view, Michael Mays describes the characters in the *Wake* as 'manifestations of specific and local (often extremely local) historical energies positioned within a range of intersecting and overlapping relationships' (Mays 1998, 25). Joyce's language operates as a technics of globalisation, in that it is the result of language corrupting and reconfiguring itself under the pressure of multiple language types, and it turns these pressures into a form of release and freedom. Indeed, reading the *Wake* as a struggle with internalised externalities provides instructive echoes between Joyce's and Breeze's unwieldy codified languages. That is, the language operates as a textural signifier of struggle and difficulty at the convergence of social forces, a technics for speaking truth beneath detection and a method for producing new linguistic imaginaries.

Modernist Author as Proto-Computer

One of the instructive aspects of reading early modernist and later experimental code works together is that such reading invites us to envisage the artist as a proto-computer, manually executing laborious processes that will one day be automated and subsequently internalised as a habit. The complex linguistic forms authors such as Beckett and Joyce found by intensifying then-latent aspects of the world finds echoes in the forms linguistic technologies have taken since. Years later, the internalised language of the reader and cognitive worker, alienated and compelled by a language that is only partly their own, resonates with Beckett's and Joyce's 'experimental' literary gestures, making them realist in ways that contemporaneous analysis would not have anticipated.

That is to say, the effect of reading modernist and artificial intelligence works together is that the proto-realism of the earlier works, entirely written by a human author, offers a glimpse at the mechanics of the computational forms of cognition that increasingly dictate our own working and thinking. The tensions between semi-automated speech and action, and the body's resistance that we see in *Watt*, and the fluid, deeply 'real-time' language of *Finnegan's Wake,* both evoke sentiments contained in recent science fiction and speculative writing. The humanoid robot who narrates Kazuro Ishiguro's novel *Klara in the Sun* (2021), for example, sees the world in fragmented ways that problematise her interactions with it and that feel strangely *Watt*-like:

> 'Klara', the Mother said in a firmer voice, and suddenly she'd become partitioned into many boxes, far more than at the Friend's Apartment when the Father had first come in. In several of the boxes her eyes were narrow, while in others they were wide open and large. In one box there was room only for a single staring eyeball. I could see parts of Mr Capaldi at the edges of some boxes, so I was aware that he'd raised his hand into the air in a vague gesture. (Ishiguro 2021, 39)

The unsettled, difficult and remixed lexicon of Joyce, in turn, anticipates the call for a posthuman language by Braidotti and Hlavajova: 'new notions and terms [that] are needed to address the constituencies and configurations of the present and to map future directions' (2016, 1). As we saw in chapter 1, the Urban Dictionary and the personalisable dictionary of auto-text functions are instances where media apparatuses have adapted to absorb the errant lexicons of new social vernaculars emerging from the Anthropocene, of the kinds we see in Joyce's work.

What I would like to turn to now are some contemporary instances of the kind of language hybrids and language machines proposed by Beckett and Joyce, looking in experimental literature for glitchy-realist modes that articulate the 'rough terrain' of working while subjected to digital and digital-age alienation. In the remaining part of this chapter, I want to show how automated language produces glitch-like error behaviours in ways anticipated by formal experiments with the novel that are now captured in artwork outside of the literary field.

The Mediatised Workplace

Working-class work is no longer undertaken in structurally distinctive places to middle-class work, as it was during the last industrial revolution. Still, the intensity of the virtual and actual environments we work in and our subjection to the 'temporal traumata' of the digital (Ernst 2018) diverge hugely dependent on class. Whereas the factory or mine were homogenous and hermetically sealed off from the outside world, today's call centres, fulfilment centres, gyms, hairdressers, food halls and supermarkets are spaces that are infested by the real-time, real-world presence of media entertainment, performance management and data retrieval, and heavily scripted modes of interaction (Anandarajan and Simmers 2018). Labourers are monitored, their activity determined and regimented to algorithmic degrees of efficiency, and the work environment is peppered with brand-specific media content: local radio, advertising, staff-and-customer announcements. The open-plan office also differs from the factory floor in the way it is hybridised with the outside and in the fluidity between social and working hours. Cognitive labourers in this environment often moonlight in the emotional and 'sharing' economy during work hours or breaks, *cyber-loafing* on the company internet (Lim 2002) by posting on their social media and dating accounts on work time. Socialising during work time is not discouraged, in part because sociality is one of the new extractive modes of capitalism in service industry jobs.

In *A Grammar of the Multitude,* Paolo Virno describes the contemporary worker as a 'virtuoso' whose social improvisation is monetised in the workplace: 'the tasks of a worker or of a clerk no longer involve the completion of a single particular assignment, but the changing and intensifying of social cooperation' (2001, 13). The virtuoso labourer internalises a 'common language' for performing their role within capitalism. Still, this common language is analogous to the systematic discipline of mechanical machines in previous eras, translating sociality into a product by twisting and intensifying certain repetitive aspects. As with the alien languages of the digital, Virno frames social performance in extractive terms, as a kind of colonisation of the public conscious: 'Nobody is as poor as those who see their own relation to the presence of others, that is to say, their own communicative faculty, their own possession of a language, reduced to wage labour' (Virno 2001, 65). It is perhaps in the exaggerated slangs and slurs of digital-age vernacular that we can best detect the emergence of Chun's notion of 'public habituation' to the temporalities of media (Chun 2014): the scars of the newly conjoined social-work space. The twin fragmentation of the working class by globalisation and the workplace by the 'creepy' intrusion of media and managerialism into the private sphere has resulted in a heterogeneous language condition shot through with strange temporalities, lags, gaps, anomalies and intensities. Glitches are moments in which the intense weaves of media, unconscious scripting of sociality, and leisure and non-work interests spasm and come into conflict with one another, causing 'the cognitive switching costs' (Berry 2012) or even 'digital orgasms' (Russell 2020) that form part of the texture of the working day.

Video work by Ryan Trecartin (2012) deploys glitched language as a vernacular 'action' that articulates the result of communicative faculties being subjected to the rates and intensities of computational technology. Trecartin coaches the actors for his films with oddly formatted written scripts (fig. 17) that contain telling vernacular 'errors' that collapse different kinds of word meanings (such as 'Pieaece').*

These performances are then post-produced using time-shift and sharp edits, making each scene into a frantic language event. His work addresses the intensities of sociality and professionalism in the entertainment industry, but also the financialisation of social interaction embodied in the ways social media is used for 'status', which is then monetised. The films are invariably populated by adult-child 'tweens' reminiscent of reality TV celebrities, who oscillate between libidinous and disinterested, voicing mixtures of internal and internal dialogue in a kind of internalised internet-meme and marketing-inspired slang. As with the current trend for the social media platform TikTok, it is never really clear whether the characters are performing for camera or being caught on candid footage.

00:28:42

(VOY):	Don't talk 2me Behind my **FRONT.**

FRONT⊖

(VOY):	**BASIC'ly** ,When i'm older, you're gonna **wish i'wasn't.** : **i want** you **to get Bored in'a'Band** with **ME.** if i'wer an .idiot!, i'd-be drinking O.J. **i want** my MOMs **to get Bored and'abandon ME.**
(VOY)**Ceader:**	Good Thing. I'm **Gay**. Because My MOM'a **Collection.** Is **INappropriate.**
Jordan (MD):	When i Think about **YOU.**
(VOY)**Ceader:**	i do got good **(i's).**
Tracy (MD):	Ceader?
(VOY)**Ceader:**	**FactOR.**
Tracy (MD):	Why's my'side of the BEDroom Smaller than HERs?
Jordan (MD):	Tracy?
(VOY)**Ceader:**	FUCK, Shut the Fuck UP - ***MOM***! x!(#*
Tracy (MD):	Jordan.
(VOY)**Ceader:**	FRUACK!
Jordan (MD):	Dance'ie
Tracy (MD):	U Never x!(#* Look @ME_ it's Just NOT x!(#* something u DO x!(#* anymore
(VOY)**Ceader:**	ffuck x!(#*
Jordan (MD):	You're a NEED x!(#*U need2 x!(#* Go find your'self x!(#* a NEEDER......Focus on CEADER.
(VOY)**Ceader:**	u'no? .... **Yetever.** 'UCK Trading Same Places */TAKE
(VOY):	**Pie*ae*ce a WAY!**
(VOY)**Ceader:**	King Size !PROMO,

Fig. 17. Unedited extract from the script for Ryan Trecartin's The Re'Search (Re'Search Wait'S), 2009-10, 00:28:42–00:32:19. Used with permission.

Trecartin describes his approach to creating the frenetic language texture in his films as 'accepting the flux of things rather than the definition or container' (De Wachter 2012, 55), and, indeed, there are frequent moments where words are used as placeholders for actions, and vice versa, with emphasis on context and energy transfer between characters. Dialogues consist of high-speed aphorisms sewn together into a continual spew that oscillates between meaningless and pointed, striated with affecting jolts of register. Again, as with Sutherland's and Scourti's response to the techno-linguistic situation, rather than the fragment, the organising principle of these kludged conversations is the pressurised 'leak', 'bloom' or 'splurge'.

One interpretation is that the films are a dramatisation of a particular, perhaps hysterical, internet zone where comments, likes and hyperbole rule. Words speak themselves out of the characters' mouths, the inhuman speed of their delivery pushing their relation to us to its limits. The slip is crucial in this context, revealing the unconscious bias of the speaker. In one section of *Centre Jenny* (2013), a character sitting in a technospiritual-induced daze produces iterations of a phrase: 'You might end up in touch with the source. You might end up *with* in touch with the source...' This minor grammatical slip – one among many in the film – becomes the subject of a highly productive indeterminacy. Is 'in touch with the source' something you are ('you might end up [being] in touch with the source') or, in this world, is it a commodity ('you might end up *with* In-Touch-With-The-Source')? In the world of *Centre Jenny*, this phrase suggests, ownership and being – like human and technofinancial determination – are split along a flickering, indeterminate relation. In Trecartin's films capital has exhausted the conscious and colonises the unstable unconscious realm beyond: the 'Freudian slip' becomes indistinguishable from the catchphrase; nonsense indistinguishable from the irruption of a new truth.

The theme of unconsciously absorbed media is also at the centre of *The Unspeakable Freedom Device,* a 2015 video work[29] by Jennet Thomas which deals extensively with the shifting and glitching of boundaries between human and technological language as our interface with the world. The characters in *The Unspeakable Freedom Device* exist in a post-apocalyptic (and post-digital) rural environment whose prehistory indicates a radical internalisation of the informatic condition. The 'collapsing signs and imploding meanings' of language (Hayles 2010) are flickeringly apparent in how the characters interact with sigil-like technologies embedded in otherwise strangely bucolic surroundings as they take a pilgrimage to a party-political conference. Throughout the film, what should be solely linguistic metaphors go beyond the metaphysical role of meaning and are executed on the body. Much of Thomas's work touches on a kind of slippage between what should be metaphysical (or, for example, the immaterial operations of code) and the material world. The slippage between metaphysical and physical is achieved in Thomas's video work through a kind of glitch poetics in which metaphors have material consequences for her characters. The metaphorical-real slippage is perhaps most disturbingly reflected in the prehistory of the 'red worker' characters, whose hands have literally withered and dropped off in the face of an unnamed 'semiotic onslaught': 'their useless hands shamefully exposed to raw unfiltered awareness' (Thomas 2015). This glitchy slippage is reinforced by the frequent reverse and cut-up effects on voices when characters speak in the film, as though the characters have internalised a glitching 'device'. It is the flickering, glitching relation between the linguistic and the material that the titular Freedom Device proposes to do away with completely, as the salesman/politico Blue John proclaims in the closing scenes: 'Eternal BLUE, beyond all fluctuations – Unspeakable Freedom!'.

Blue is, of course, the colour of neoliberals, the Conservative party in the UK, but it is also the colour informally used to represent the digital. Thomas imagines the device as the ultimate techno-linguistic app: a computational prosthesis, producing in its user-hosts the phenomenon of being 'free' while 'always working', and thus being enslaved to cognitive labour. This image provides a commentary on today's social-work situation in which companies extract value from the data and emotional and mental energy people expend in their social interactions. In a neat reflection of the *fait acompli* of Silicon Valley's relationship to its customer base, the device is 'advertised' to attendees assembled at the political conference at the same time as it is revealed that it has already been implanted.

Language Compulsion in Performance

It is not surprising, given the default formal vernacular of literary publishing, that the realist glitches of the contemporary creative workspace can be found written most effectively outside of the novel. Performance also does not require the networks that the comparatively middle-class dominated world of novel publishing does. The poems and modes of speaking encountered in performance spaces are less refined and less rarefied than literary 'circles', often including gaps where the audience or a sound component can splinter into the work and integrate verbal ticks to replicate the motions and latencies of media portals.

In David J's 'Bullets Were Baptised' (2008), the poet tells a story from multiple viewpoints in a way that recalls hyper-sensationalised and hyper-mediated television shows such as *CSI Miami*, vividly evoking a bullet reentering a gun in slow motion, the smoke in reverse, and integrating skip, echo and rewind 'effects' with his voice. This is a kitsch 'effect', but effective nonetheless in combination with the other aspects of the performance. Perhaps the most striking of these is the presence of meta-monologues narrating the poem, also performed by the poet in difference voices, speaking to himself about the space he is in, reflecting and commenting on aspects of the story often in a mixture of different registers. The effect is a kind of shimmering, troubled paranoia, a form of realism that combines the violence and suspicion of YouTube 'truther' videos and crime dramas with the languages of advertising, pop music and informal conversation, as though encountered through multiple bedroom and ceiling walls. To me, the glitches in David J's poems evoke the challenges and distractions of communal work- and living- spaces, insecurity and spectacle, and when he jams his domestic situation with the internalisation of media as a stylistic effect, the resulting hybrid has a political bite.[30]

In a different kind of performance, Mark Greenwood also reflects on the social intensities of hybrid work and leisure spaces through their bearing on language 'acts'. Greenwood integrates and folds multiple types of language into his work, using a motif of 'inscription': the act of writing that leaves marks on environments, materials and people. In his work, people inscribe and are inscribed by language actions, causing feedback loops of repeated actions that give rise to maddening effects, complicating and intensifying the language situation. *Lad Broke* (2012) is a 48-hour performance in which Greenwood draws on his experience as a day manager in a Ladbrokes bookmaker's, appropriating the language actions of this space to reflect on compulsive behaviours of the professional gambler and casualised service sector worker.

For 48 hours on the Grand National weekend, Greenwood stations himself at a small table, dressed in a long dark coat, copying out winning horses' names from gambling receipts onto betting slips. Once he has written a horse's name, he throws the small red pen he has used to the floor and pins the slip onto a pentagram of elastic bands strung across the space. An absurdist poem of horse names forms in the ceiling space, and a visual poem of red 'cuts' forms on the floor. Both of these poetic gestures linked to the gambling motif of the work ironically detourn the notion of 'chance operation' common in avant-garde poetry. The script is already written, of course, by last weekend's horse winners, printed by the bookie's clerk earlier that week, but by pinning the words up for examination the space becomes rich with happenstance linguistic meetings. Victoria Gray's description captures some other elements of the situation:

> [A] recording of fierce commentary from thoroughbred racehorse Red Rum's five Grand Nationals (1973-1977) provides an ominous temporal pulse; underpinning and fuelling the work's dynamic tensions. As Greenwood occasionally switches the record player between its twin speeds we move into and out of paces; peaks and troughs affect the heart rate, actively shifting the stakes at play. On the floor methodically placed sheets of newspaper form a grid structure, all detailing statistical betting information. The grid, not just an aesthetic component, proposes a choreographic structure of corridors with which Greenwood negotiates a variety of careful ritual pathways. This choreographic and poetic taxonomy of numbers and names sits below the canopy of words bearing the names of winning horses. The lighthearted titles flirt with each other; above and below us they provide comical and ironic juxtapositions, diverting our attentions from what is really at stake, the body. (Gray 2012)

For Greenwood's 'character' then, the writing body is caught in 'ritual pathways' between a moribund inevitability and an almost heroic contingency. As though to swing the balance, at points Greenwood breaks with his writing to perform ritual actions of ambiguous symbolic quality: nailing a horseshoe to a wall, beating his head against a door frame, blowing up red balloons in front of his face before pinging them across the room, and, finally, cutting the words of the work's title, 'LAD' and 'BROKE', into his chest with a razor. Each of these elements – sound, writing, ritual action – are worked with as language forms, the play of the inscribing and inscribed body, capturing the compulsions that we accept in subjection to the contingencies of work.

The central character of Greenwood's action could be a bookmaker driven to distraction by the intensities and repetitions of thinking, doing, stress, release, downfall in his workplace; or the dream-like versioning of a gambler caught in rituals of superstition, betting and coping mechanism. In either instance, the inference is that the 'virtuoso' acts of labour and leisure low down the social scale glitch the body and mind into simple loops that are impossibly arduous in their duration and insistence. The way the industrial worker was measured by the piece-rate of a machine has morphed into a more insidious situation where the contemporary body is subjected to the loops and contingencies of computable signs.

Broken, gappy and corrupted language practices such as those of Trecartin, Thomas, David J and Greenwood suggest that there should be apposite techniques for representing the unique situation for contemporary work in the novel today. But there are boundaries eliding language error (and the people who write it) from the literary mainstream. There is a gap between the post-human imaginaries of today's 'social science-fiction' (a term which has been used of Trecartin's work), Joyce's and Beckett's engagement in code and hybridised language forms, and the realist glitches of autofiction, in which the contemporary workplace is articulated as a linguistic intensity. Structural and aesthetic reasons have, for the most part, brought a particular latency to the emergence of this kind of fiction.

Expressionist Realism and the Worker Monologue

Ironically perhaps, one of the most astute novelists of the mediatised working-class vernacular wrote about this condition most memorably in a period novel that fictionalises the end of the industrial era for the country, and from the vantage point of Tokyo. David Peace's *GB84* (2004) is a novel about the miners' strikes of 1984 and the unforgiving government-sponsored violence, subterfuge and familial collapse that ended it. Peace is known for his deployment of repetitious prose to emblematise hard work or to build narrative tensions. In this novel, the repetition is there, but Peace also writes through a combination of literary styles, all of them stripped bare of emotional reflection or omniscient separation from the events as lived and glitched together, like the bands of interference on a broken television. Dramatic monologue in dialect and hard-boiled narrative prose are combined with lines from news-reportage, fragments of half-listened to dialogue and internal monologue, and sonic signatures – the haunting *'krk-krk'* of the police batons, omnipresent, whether hit against heads or shields and the oddly ambiguous 'Click click' of a tapped telephone wire – are combined page-to-page with a highly affecting astringent, repetitious hardness. As Mark Fisher has noted, 'the result is more poetic than most poetry; it is, naturally, a poetry stripped of all lyricism, a harshly dissonant word-music' (Fisher 2018).

In this extract, the poetic method is used to render the almost musical inevitability of events placed 'under control' by one of the bourgeois characters (himself a playwright), including the title of a misremembered Bertold Brecht play:

> The closing of a pit and the calling of a strike –
>
> The lighting of a corridor. The shadow on a wall –
>
> Fear and Misery in this New Reich.
>
> Neil Fontaine stands outside the Jew's suite. He listens to the toasts – Inside.
>
> (Peace 2004, 16)

The internal monologues of the central working-class characters are less straightforward, unrelenting in their fragmented, distracted quality, at once utterly introspective and inseparable from the cognitive and physical violence of the outside world. A miner called Martin, whose wife eventually leaves him, narrates battles with police and with his own conscience. His waking world a kind of shutter-stock of nightmare visions, his dreams cut into unsettling Old English chants:

> Orgreave. Fucking Orgreave. Here we go. Here we go. Here we go – Here I go down. Here I go under. Here I get lost – I get kiss of life and a fractured fucking skull. Day 89. They keep us in for observation. Daft bastard fell off a ladder, that's what Pete tells doctors. Fell off a ladder and down stairs. They send us home after twenty-four hours. Bag of bandages. Load of pills. Plenty of rest. Doctor's orders – Rest. Sleep. Rest. Sleep – I lie here in our big bed. ... I lie here and I listen to rain on our windows. To her tears – I turn over. I look at her – Her hopes. Her fears – All our hopes. All our fears – I close my eyes. Tight – Under the ground, we brood. *We hwisprian. We onscillan.* Under the ground, we scream – I open my eyes. Wide – She's not finished with us. Not finished with any of us. (Peace 2004, 276)

The 'expressionist realism' (Fisher 2018) glitching montage effect of the novel is further energised and textured by the inclusion of lyrics from songs from the charts that year: the first half of the book uses Nena's 'Ninety-Nine Red Balloons', and the second uses Frankie Goes to Hollywood's 'Two Tribes Go to War', and later there is George Michael's 'Careless Whisper' and the Live Aid song 'Do They Know it is Christmas'. The effect of this is to throw the bubble-gum world of 1980s pop into stark contrast with the material existence of the miners while rendering the weird omnipresence of emotive language, emptied of its original significance and latched onto by a distracted conscious. In the case of the first two, the Cold War context of the lyrics is ironically, bitterly, detourned to refer to the internecine war fought by the miners: 'Turn the radio on for the rest of the way. *Two Tribes* – Must have heard that bloody song ten times a day now for weeks. Ought to make it bloody National Anthem, said Sean' (Peace 2004, 434). The radio is not a luxury or entertainment but part of the texture of a cognitively inhospitable world. In fact, the media itself detourns – in this extract 'stitches' and 'stitches-up' – events:

> The nation was outraged –
>
> Not by the assault on the miner. Not by the assault on the President. No –
>
> The TV had lied again. They had cut the film. They had stitched it back together –
>
> Stitched up the Union with it –
>
> Miners threw stones. Miners hurt horses. Miners rioted –
>
> '– the worst industrial violence since the war –'
>
> Police defended themselves. Police upheld the law. Police contained the riot –
>
> That was it.
>
> (Peace 2004, 343)

Reading *GB84's* stitchings and affective montage effects, we can retrospectively attribute the 1980s with the accelerated, 'post-truth', hypermediated atmosphere that is well documented today. The tensions of Peace's prose style are partly the result of his writing habits. Peace is known to play the records from the era he is depicting on a loop while writing. As with other authors who consciously mediatise their work environment (such as Hart Crane, who similarly played his gramophone on a loop while writing poetry [Reed 2004, 104]), this method allows the writer to access the qualities still latent in the media of that era. Reading *GB84* (or in fact any of Peace's intensely repetitious prose works), I think of nothing so much as the twenty-first-century labourer, working to call-time limits, clicking between corporate scripts and 24-hour news feeds, Facebook feeds of asinine life advice, Microsoft Excel, cut and paste pdfs, virus popups… a cognitive subject cut adrift from their social solidarity and given multifaceted emotional labour toys in return.

Other novelists have taken up this mode of pressured writing in direct evocation of the workplace. Richard Makin's *Concussion Protocols* (2019) is an example that cites the novel form in its structure and pushes into it more expressionist language, whose texture evokes the information worker:

> The retail where she worked slash died was a
> poisonous mass of incompetence and sabotage.
> It can only be assumed that they bring the
> remembrance of their species with them into
> each new existence – that is, they have preserved

> memories of what was experienced by their ancestors. I remember that final day.
>
> She looked at me in the half-light.
>
> 'Did you see it splitting? Did you see your spine going scream?'
>
> (Makin 2019, 12)

As Iain Sinclair says of this book, the result is an 'assault on our conditioned reflexes' and that it is Makin's 'refusal to capitulate to the protocols of [literary] history' (Makin 2019, cover quote) that give the work its contemporary purchase. Glitches and other disruptive innovations in Peace's and Makin's work are the distorted, anachronistic future reflections that diagram new cognitive space for the working-class novel.

Conclusion

Ultimately, thinking through glitch as a literary realism, and realism as an environment where the implications of emergent media can be played out as a component of social forces, sets the stage for understanding literary disrupters alongside technological innovations producing new forms of connectivity out of unforeseen but pre-existing vectors. If the struggles, fragmentations and intensities of the contemporary moment are felt particularly keenly by the working class, then it is in the poetics of intensity and disruption, which I call glitch poetics, that new affinities can be formed. As I have suggested with regard to the work of Scourti and Bergvall, I recognise the potential for new forms of solidarity and affinity to emerge in the glitch as it reactivates media conditions as shared experience, where reading difficulty produces emotive and material connections between the reader and writerly conditions. Undoubtedly, literature continues to be dominated by people whose experience of the media environment is distinctively benign, but there is evidence in para-literary approaches such as performance writing where media's latent characteristics find stranger and more aggressively 'real' forms of expression and purchase on the world.

Conclusion

Connecting Errors

Poetry is the introduction of error and dysfunctionality into language, producing excess affect, surprising aesthetics and styles, and gaps into which critical and alternative thinking can take place. In the instance of glitch poetics, the aesthetics and critical perspectives offered relate to the intersection of language and technology. What I have sought to do in this book is document a range of ways in which affective and critical language practices probe the digital. I have also attempted to illustrate how the insights gained from reading these errors push against and bleed into discoveries made in 'more digital' disciplines.

I have frequently implied that distinct words, qualities, styles and tropes are 'glitched together'. But what does this mean? 'Glitched together' is a synonym of *mixed*, as in the instance where liquids and oils can be said to be mixed for as long as they are being stirred or shaken together, but also *jammed*, where things are pushed together so they crush and interleave, and *kludged*, meaning incompatibilities that are connected and made to work 'in a pinch'. When things are mixed, jammed or kludged, they produce an ambiguous, temporary state or form, and a range of unexpected results. The glitch is a space of ambiguity and hybridity that moves and iterates by requiring immediate responses; it is a paradoxical, travelling boundary space where established forms of interaction and definition are untied and retangled. Curt Cloninger notes that one of the main ways that language glitches do this is by breaking down the dichotomy between what words mean and the sensations produced by their material appearance: glitched language is overloaded with 'affective' sensation of the body, throat, screen, alphabet and syntax, through which it says anything at all. The moment we encounter a glitched language instance, our brain's search for meaning is activated, but we find instead a weird meaning-feeling thing and are forced to make do with that. Normally, words' meanings can be unpicked from how they make us feel, but in glitch poetics, feeling and meaning remain deeply entangled. Roy Claire Potter talks about the errors in their type-written work as like 'characters' for this reason, Ben Lerner translates the sensation of the digital into a method for disturbing the surface of his texts – the sensation of corruption means something here. In these examples, form and content are hybridised and result in particularly sensuous kinds of meaning being born, with distinctive relationships to media.

Another way that glitches produce ambiguous forms is as an 'oscillation' – a rapid switching back and forth between states. Oscillation is a switch or transition that is stuck in the performance of swi*tching* back and forth.

Oscillation is a key idea for glit*ching* because it describes a mode in which the temporalities of a medium outrun perceptive capacity and produce ambiguous, strange, ghostly and illusory effects. Like a thaumatrope illusion, where the persistence of human vision blends the images on two sides of a rapidly spinning piece of card into a single image, the glitch oscillation produces an effect in the receiver that is temporary and virtual, yet 'real' and absorbing. Berry notes that oscillation is one of the key qualities of how media work through errors, oscillating between crash and recovery, processing and display, in rapid succession, just below our perceptive limits. He suggests that our attention also oscillates: the rapid process-display ontology of computers repeats as a pattern in our conscious as multiple tabs, notifications, crashes and priorities pull at and release our attention. In this book, I have documented numerous oscillations happening in language: the rapid switching between poetic images and poetic registers in Keston Sutherland's lyrics; the brain's perceptive attention being drawn between Erica Scourti's voice and the text of a speed reader animation in *Negative Docs*; the simultaneous evocations made by the portmanteau of Mez Breeze and James Joyce, sensation-like images or concepts that vibrate in multiply evocative word-objects.

Seeking to reflect the oscillation and hybrid qualities that result from glitches between media and language, the writing in this book has itself oscillated between, and hybridised, different subject matters and concepts. The book is a consciously kludgy attempt at producing glitch poetics out of an oscillation between literary and media analysis. It is an idea somewhere between a concept and a practice of writing. Glitch poetics functions here as a mode of reading and a subject of that reading, a manner of literature found inside, among and blended with the media sphere, a blended space of gesture and style with language and a symptom of the present technological condition. What I hope to have done is to have slowed down and identify the different components of this idea, and shown how it is already present in different fields, before accelerating them somewhat into hybrid interpretations. Throughout this book I use a mixture of technical and literary close reading, and anecdotal and reportage in historical and speculative modes, demonstrating the meshing of technologies, ideologies and forms of relation in the current moment. The fast-moving nature of the digital in the age we live in demands a similarly rapidly evolving notion of the glitch. Accordingly, the book historicises its most recent case studies and does not account for developments in artificial intelligence and blockchain technology that are dominating current discourse. That is a matter for another book.

Glitch Poetics is a work of the digital aesthetics of the last decade, finding that the digital has saturated our environments and infested our consciousness to the degree that it can be found in the styles and textures of 'non-digital' literature. What I show concerning various language works, poems and prose practices of the 2010s is that in the literature of this moment the digital manifests itself in ways we experience as error. Language is corrupted by the digital and corruptions in language evoke distinctive aspects of our lives within the digital context. Glitch is a useful term because it speaks specifically to the dominant digital contexts and allows for the ambiguities between cause and effect of error – whether corrupted textures are the result of technical mistakes or simply the product of something exceeding our limited expectations – to be suspended. What is important is the sensation and the kinds of knowledge and alterity instigated by errors in language.

The book is also a work of literary criticism, starting with close readings of textures of alterity and technical corruption in poetry and prose. But I have allowed my analysis to expand outward and seek purchase on the world via readings of media devices, often in conversation with media art. This mode of criticality contributes to the development of interdisciplinary perspectives, in particular a dialogue between technical and creative cultures, by showing how shared media contexts provide a basis for cross-readings of literature and the wider cultural sphere. Poetry in particular has been largely sidelined in the discussion of advances in technology and many would say that it has sidelined itself with a conceptual asceticism, restricting its purview to the goings-on of language rather than tying these to the wider circulation of language in today's contexts. As I hope I have begun to show here, media errors offer one mode of purchase literary analysis can use to link textual experiments with today's lived (media) realities.

By applying the term 'glitch' to disciplines beyond media art, I have sought to broaden it in a way that traces potentials without sacrificing the particular potency of the term. I have qualified this gesture by demonstrating how the ways of delineating the territory for glitch – for example, glitches as phenomena occurring between digital and non-digital forms, or glitch as a term specific to new media cultures – themselves imply formal boundaries with the literary that do not hold up in practice. There are continuities between cultures of esoteric literature and those that produce software, and the necessarily 'digital' quality of writing as a system of discontinuous elements that each operates tension with literary writing. Glitch poetics is the result of these tensions turning into a style or a critical perspective.

It is unlikely that many of the writers whose work I analyse in this book care particularly about digital mechanics such as the 'micro-temporal processes' happening within computers, but I conclude that the digital quality of their works results from the fact that their composition process is open to the world that has been affected by the digital. Rather than containing any purposefully integrated knowledge about digital technologies, knowledge about these technologies results from the kinds of reading the poems instigate. The literary works discussed in the book are also attempts to know. I have attempted to answer the demands of this condition for literature by pairing readings of poems with readings of media devices, and by drawing together a range of observations from software studies, poetics, and media theory. It is clear to me that the posthumanities research environment as a whole needs to allow itself to be shaped by the kinds of hybridity its artworks – and glitches – display if we are to understand them fully.

By applying ideas from media art to contemporary poetics, I have also concertedly tried to open up the range of things that can be written about when we consider such terms as 'new media poetics', 'digital poetics' and 'digital poetry'. Currently the academic work around these terms tends to be compromised by a heavy emphasis on platforms, and on 'clickable' forms of interaction, rather than on literary heritage and affect. Language is more closely intertwined with the operation of digital media than it was with the previously dominant media forms, and this sets the stage for a particular kind of critical media poetics that is not platform-specific. It even presents a new opportunity to read back into literary histories.

My readings and theoretical discussions inevitably end with a reflection on the aesthetic effect of encountering glitch poetics practices. I suggest that, along with the disruptive quality of glitches that we find in the texts under analysis, glitches open up particular nodes of intimacy and empathy between authors and readers. Examples of this include the way Bergvall's poem 'About Face' emphasises the subvocalisation mechanisms in our faces as we read it, or the intensely moving way that the interior monologues of David Peace's characters are retemporalised and twisted by the rigours of being on strike, infected by the saccharine, cruelly ironic world of popular media and the way in which the author's language produces this same dissemblance in us. Glitch poetics communicate something recognisably – perhaps surprisingly – 'emotive' about the contemporary condition of the digital in a paradoxically unreal fashion and this invites us to understand at a more fundamental level than meaning. As I suggest of Samuel Beckett's, James Joyce's, Ryan Trecartin's and Jennet Thomas' work, it is the combination of the seemly inevitable increase of the intensity of digital aesthetics in our everyday life and the propensity of artists to exaggerate and amplify our experience of these aesthetics as they currently are that give glitch poetics its speculative quality.

In an accompanying collection of poems, available to download and view on the Open Humanities Press website, I have attempted to trace the possibilities for glitch poetics as a consciously used literary device. The poems are included here because they hopefully add some colour to a question that haunts this book: what if someone knew they were writing glitch poetics? The poems were produced over a series of years while I wrote this book. Overlaid across the poems in the collection, and viewable as an animated series on the OUP website, is a series of portmanteau that the Torch-RNN 'artificial intelligence' came up with after reading *Glitch Poetics*. This late addition reflects my increasingly strong conviction that the glitch is a vital method for productive collaborations with recent developments in natural language processing. The 'wrongly spelt' but evocative concepts invented by the poorly trained AI in this case each sketch a possible concept for future elaboration, the fragile, perhaps silly edges of digital authorship that are often forgotten in the quest for ever-more high-fidelity copies of human writing.

Within the pamphlet itself, each of the text works addresses glitch poetics as a practical method for writing across and through media, and looking for different affective properties in error. For example, to produce '*Silence May Be Kept*', I corrupted a source text, the Anglican 'Compline' prayer by shifting each syllable in a systematic way, using spreadsheet software. This technique was influenced by the method of 'pixel drifting' in glitch art cultures. 'Whorls I & II' also made use of spreadsheet software to reorder and glitch their original source, but in this case, I wrote directly into the spreadsheet, and the text is broken up into units of line and image. A sequence called 'Scripts for a Working Class Play' is produced with other desktop software, and readers will recognise the presence of mark-up, columns and tabular features used to glitch the texts in what I hope is an unconventional fashion, evoking what I have referred to in this book as the intensely mediatised environments of today's working lives. Other poems, such as 'Our Only Encounter', fold together multiple glitching techniques, visual and conceptual, with some of the theoretical language from this book, make use of translation software or take-up the glitch as a method for troubling image and narrative voice – as in 'Shadow Fountain'. I hope that this book and the poetry pamphlet, taken together, will encourage more in-depth future explorations – and offer a useful way of thinking about, reading and writing the cultures of the contemporary moment through the productive misuse of literary techné.

Notes

1 This is an approximation based on a presentation and publication on audio synthesis by Brian House (2017).

2 A sample of news headlines taken in Spring 2021 that use the term 'glitch'.

3 This is based on artwork and critical writing by Pip Thornton (2019).

4 See also Nicolas Maiget's *Pirate Cinema* (2012-14, https://thepiratecinema.com) for a work that makes 'available for aesthetic exploration the pre-existing potentials of Peer-to-Peer architectures' as a glitch aesthetic.

5 Brown and Kutty (2012) use a discussion of Murata's work to describe how the compression-decompression (codec) mechanisms of digital video work: 'When the data that make up a film are compressed to fit onto a DVD, ... that original 20gb is discarded. Typically, this involves keeping all of the data from prominent, or key, frames (hence the term "keyframes", which can also be referred to as i- or image-frames ...). However, for the frames between keyframes, commonly referred to as p-frames, only the aspects of the image that have changed (e.g. pixels whose colour value has shifted) are kept, the unchanged aspects/pixels being made simply to refer back to the same colour value in the keyframe' (163). They also describe how these mechanics are taken advantage of to produce the *datamoshing* technique of Murata and others: 'The artists use the changing elements of the p-frames that arise when video files are compressed and they add these to i-frames from different digital moving images, with the result that the i-frame of one image, typically paused momentarily on screen, suddenly seems to

dematerialise as the moving aspects of the p-frames from another moving image begin to manifest themselves on, within or from behind it' (168).

6 See also Menkman's collaboration with Johan Larsby, *Monglot* (2011), https://beyondresolution.info/Monglot.

7 In chapter 3, I pursue this analogy, exploring how working-class everyday speech differentiates from the default 'formal vernacular' of most public speech and so is registered as error – and how this affects and turns into a literary imperative in the UK scene in particular.

8 In chapter 2, I look at the work of Baudelaire during this period, and specifically his use of confusion and the blizzard of snow motifs to evoke the 'dissembling' public quality of the new urban spaces, foreshadowing the rearranged, corrupted poetry of an era of online public spaces.

9 Fran Locke (2021) and Jeff T. Johnson (2019) offer two other perspectives on combinations of error and media materiality in today's experimental language practice, particularly in relation to class.

10 Summarising the concerns of Bernard Stiegler (in *Technics and Time* [1998]), Kember and Zylinska agree that, although technics themselves are inseparable from what is human, 'a radical change has taken place over the last century, with the speed of technological transformation and intensity of technical production constantly increasing and getting ahead of the development of other spheres of life' (2015, 16).

11 This is an observation made by Vit Bohal in the introduction to Ames Čermák's 2020 experiemental fiction *returnself.new:* 'programming language provides a mirror for the natural languages and the relationship between ritual (as a set protocol of symbolic actions) and machine algorithm (i.e. an automated sequence of computational tasks) is no longer as distant – both social ritual and contemporary technology are based on the repeated iteration of operations which are built on a progressive law or syntax (linguistic, machinic, cultural…)' (in Cerak 2020, 6).

12 In his recent essay on 'esolangs', 'What Programming Language Would Yoko Ono Create', Temkin (2021) demonstrates that faulty, difficult to use, bespoke coding languages are themselves art works as forms of language invention.

13 This is a reference to two instances where Serra's works have caused harm. In 1971 Richard Johnson, a 34-year-old labourer installing Serra's work was killed when the sculpture toppled over; 18 years later, another worker lost a leg in a similar accident.

14 Though Steven Hammer (2013), Curt Cloninger (2010) and Olga Goriunova and Alexi Shulgin (2008) have connected the glitch project to historical experimental literature or contemporary language practices with media, their work does not include analysis of contemporary literary practices.

15 In my paper 'My Monstuices Composer' I address the topic of 'artificial intelligence' in natural language processing, arguing that if an AI were able to produce new concepts, it would likely be in a form of glitch poetics.

16 According to the United Nations Office for Disaster Risk Reductions, there has been a rise in climate-related disasters during the past twenty years. Between 1980 and 1999, there were 3,656 climate-related events, as opposed to 6,681 between 2000 and 2019. Those differences are reflected in the number of floods, which has more than doubled in the past twenty years, while the incidence of storms increased from 1,457 to 2,034.

17 Later in the book I also show how this reading resonates with the ideas of 'pre-emergence' (Williams 1977) and 'fictioning' (O'Sullivan and Burrows 2019).

18 Vladan Joler and Katie Crawford's 2020 *Anatomy of AI* diagram and paper is an example of a critical media practice engaging with the material labour and environmental costs of digital 'platforms', in this case in relation to the Amazon Echo's voice-activated assistant.

19 In this, the work recalls Bruce Nauman's 1969 work *Lip Sync.*

20 This process also echoes the creolisation of languages that resulted from English and other European nations' colonialism

in the eighteenth and nineteenth century, a resonance that I address in chapter 2.

21 Perhaps most notably, and indicating a much broader level of influence than is commonly associated with Sutherland's work, the American Pulitzer Prize-winning poet Jorie Graham repeats images, techniques and motifs of *Odes to TL61P* frequently in her 2017 collection *Fast*. In fact, her poem 'Shrouds' is composed almost entirely of unacknowledged quotations, splinters of quotation and direct references to Sutherland's work, such as 'Once I heard someone say very loudly from a podium --> the system is broken we need to fix the system --> we need to fix the system the system is broken -->' (Graham 2017,10-15). These are Sutherland's lines.

22 Aaron Kunin isolates this sentence in particular as striking in the book, saying of it: 'That last sentence is unusual in this book not just because it runs continuously past two line breaks, but also in its violent theme and public mode of address' (Kunin 2010).

23 In *The Parasite,* Michel Serres presents a prolonged engagement with the notion of distance as it is articulated, affirmed and produced by (analogue) noise: 'Perfect, successful, optimum communication no longer includes any mediation. And the canal disappears into immediacy. There would be no spaces of transformation anywhere. There are channels, and thus there must be noise' (Serres 2007, 79).

24 Jarvis was convicted of sharing child pornography images in 2017. This inexcusable crime has unfortunate resonances with the themes of Sutherland's book, but there is no intended link made here.

25 An additional echo of Wordsworth can be found in Sutherland's emphatically unpredictable approach to the poetic line, which can be read as a continuation of Wordsworth's use of blank verse in ways that combined regular line length with immense rhetorical flexibility, seen in poems such as 'The Prelude'.

26 Sean Cubitt (2015) has written about 'glitch as labour' in ways that are resonant with this aspect of Sutherland and Satrom's work.

27 There is a deliberate echo here of John Akomfrah and Edward George's film *The Last Angel of History* (1994), and its version of the Afrofuturism concept.

28 Joyce's close knowledge of and interest in the cutting-edge media and science of his day is well documented. He opened the first cinema in Dublin and his work with the 'stream of consciousness' is indebted to the nascent fact-logic description of the subconscious in Freud's psychotherapy (Gere 2016).

29 Also published as an artbook/experimental fiction by Book Works (Thomas 2015)

30 The same can be said of Hannah Silva, who also combines multi-voice works with varieties of oral glitch 'effects'.

Works Cited

Adorno, Theodor W. 1991. *Notes to Literature*. New York: Columbia University Press.

Adorno, Theodor W. 1997. *Aesthetic Theory*. London: A&C Black.

Agamben, Giorgio. 2007. 'Art, Inactivity, Politics'. In *Politics, Criticism of Contemporary Issues*. Lisbon: Fundação Serralves,131-141.

Agamben, Giorgio. 2009. *What Is an Apparatus? and Other Essays*. Stanford, CA: Stanford University Press.

Agamben, Giorgio. 2012. *Remnants of Auschwitz*. New York: Zone Books.

Andreessen, Marc. 2011. 'Why Software Is Eating the World' *Wall Street Journal*. <https://www.wsj.com/articles/SB10001424053111903480904576512250915629460> [Accessed 12 April 2021].

Antonio, Robert J. 1981. 'Immanent Critique as the Core of Critical Theory: Its Origins and Developments in Hegel, Marx and Contemporary Thought'. *The British Journal of Sociology*, 32(3): 330-345.

Artsy.net. 2014. *Takeshi Murata | Untitled (Pink Dot) (2007) | Artsy*. <https://www.artsy.net/artwork/takeshi-murata-untitled-pink-dot> [Accessed 14 February 2018].

Auerbach, Eric. 2007. *Imagine No Metaphors: The Dialectical Image of Walter Benjamin*. Imageandnarrative.be. <http://www.imageandnarrative.be/inarchive/thinking_pictures/auerbach.htm> [Accessed 7 June 2018].

Beckett, Samuel. 2009. *Watt*. London: Faber and Faber.

Benjamin, Walter. 2003. *Selected Writings*, Volume 4. Cambridge, MA: The Belknap Press.

Benjamin, Walter. 2006. *The Writer of Modern Life: Essays on Charles Baudelaire*. Cambridge, MA: Belknap Press.

Berardi, Franc. 2009. *The Soul at Work*. Los Angeles: Semiotext(e).

Berardi, Franco. 2012. *The Uprising: Poetry and Finance*. Los Angeles: Semiotext(e).

Bergvall, Caroline. 2005. *Fig*. Cambridge: Salt.

Bergvall, Caroline. 2011. *Meddle English*. Callicoon, NY: Nightboat Books.

Bergvall, Caroline. 2013. *Noping*. Triple Canopy. <https://www.canopycanopycanopy.com/contents/noping> [Accessed 19 February 2018].

Berlant, Lauren. 2016. 'The Commons: Infrastructures for Troubling Times'. *Environment and Planning D: Society and Space*, 34(3): 393-419.

Berry, David. 2011. *The Philosophy of Software*. London: Palgrave Macmillan.

Berry, David. 2012. 'Glitch Ontology'. Stunlaw.blogspot.co.uk. <http://stunlaw.blogspot.co.uk/2012/05/glitch-ontology.html> [Accessed 4 January 2018].

Bhabha, Homi K. 2012. *The Location of Culture*. London and New York: Taylor and Francis.

Bootz, Phillip. 2016. 'From OULIPO to Transitoire Observable: The Evolution of French Digital Poetry'. Dichtung-digital.org. <http://www.dichtung-digital.org/2012/41/bootz/bootz.htm> [Accessed 19 February 2018].

Boyle, Megan. 2018. *LIVEBLOG*. Rome and New York: Tyrant Books.

Braidotti, Rosi. 2013. *The Posthuman*. Oxford: Polity Press.

Braidotti, Rosi. 2016. 'The Contested Posthumanities'. Stream.liv.ac.uk. <https://stream.liv.ac.uk/jcpgctnm> [Accessed 19 February 2018].

Braidotti, Rosi and Maria Hlavajova. 2018. *The Posthuman Glossary*. London: Bloomsbury.

Breeze, Mez. 2011. *Human Readable Messages*. Vienna: Traumawien.

Briz, Nick. 2011. 'GLITCH CODEC TUTORIAL'. Nickbriz.com. <http://nickbriz.com/glitchcodectutorial/> [Accessed 12 February 2018].

Brown, Bob. 1930. *The Readies*. New York: Roving Eye Press.

Brown, William and Meetali Kutty. 2012. 'Datamoshing and the Emergence of Digital Complexity from Digital Chaos', *Convergence: The International Journal of Research into New Media Technologies*, 18(2): 165-176.

Burrows, David and Simon O'Sullivan. 2019. *Fictioning*. Edinburgh: Edinburgh University Press.

Carpenter, J. R. 2014. 'Notes on the Voyage of Owl and Girl || J. R. Carpenter'. Luckysoap.com. <http://luckysoap.com/owlandgirl/> [Accessed 24 April 2021].

Carpenter, J. R. 2016. 'etheric ocean'. Luckysoap.com. <http://luckysoap.com/ethericocean/> [Accessed 24 April 2021].

Čermák, Aleš. 2020. *returnself.new*. Prague: Alienist.

Chase, Richard. 1997. *The American Novel and its Tradition*. Baltimore: Johns Hopkins University Press.

Chun, Wendy Hui Kyong. 2016. *Updating to Remain the Same*. Cambridge, MA: MIT Press.

Cloninger, Curt and Nick Briz. 2015. 'Glitch politix Man[ual/ifesto]'. Books From The Future. <http://booksfromthefuture.tumblr.com/post/86197395718/sabotage-glitch-politix-manualifesto> [Accessed 14 February 2018].

Cloninger, Curt. 2010. 'GltchLnguistx: The Machine in the Ghost / Static Trapped in Mouths'. Lab404.com. <http://lab404.com/glitch/> [Accessed 27 February 2021].

Clune, Michael. 2016. 'The Hatred of Poetry: An Interview with Ben Lerner'. *The Paris Review*. <https://www.theparisreview.org/blog/2016/06/30/the-hatred-of-poetry-an-interview-with-ben-lerner/> [Accessed 5 January 2018].

Coates, David. 2014. 'Keston Sutherland – Odes to TL61P'. <https://davepoems.wordpress.com/2014/01/03/keston-sutherland-odes-to-tl61p/> [Accessed 17 January 2017].

Cox, Geoff and Alex Mclean. 2012. *Speaking Code: Coding as Aesthetic and Political Expression*, Cambridge, MA: MIT Press.

Craig, Elaine. 2020. 'Child's Play or Sexual Abuse? Reviewing the Efficacy of the Justice Framework in Dealing with Child on Child Sexual Abuse in the United Kingdom'. *Journal of Child Sexual Abuse*, 29(6): 734-748.

Cramer, Florian. 2005. *Words Made Flesh*. Rotterdam: Media Design Research, Piet Zwart Institute.

Cramer, Florian. 2014. 'What is Post-digital?' *A Peer Review Journal About Post-Digital Research*, [online] <http://www.aprja.net/what-is-post-digital> [Accessed 16 February 2018].

Cubitt, Sean. 2015. 'Glitch and Labour (working paper)'. Academia.edu. <https://www.academia.edu/14434817/Glitch_and_Labour_working_paper_> [Accessed 28 April 2021].

D'Aprile, Marianela. 2020. 'Delete Your Fake Account'. Jacobinmag.com. <https://jacobinmag.com/2021/02/lauren-oyler-fake-accounts-review> [Accessed 28 April 2021].

Danchev, Alex. 2011. *100 Artists' Manifestos*. London: Penguin Books.

Delville, Michel. 2013. 'Gertrude Stein's Melodies: In Anticipation of the Loop'. *Texas Studies in Literature and Language*, 55(1): 72-83.

De Wachter, Ellen Mara. Ed. 2012. *Weighted Words*. London: Zabludowicz Art Projects

Donnell, Alison and Sarah Lawson Welsh. Eds. 1996. *Routledge Reader in Caribbean Literature*. London: Routledge.

Emerson, Lori. 2014. *Reading Writing Interfaces*. Minneapolis: University of Minnesota Press.

Ernst, Wolfgang. 2017. *The Delayed Present*. Berlin: Sternberg Press.

Ferris, Natalie. 2013. 'Interview with Keston Sutherland'. <http://www.thewhitereview.org/interviews/interview-with-keston-sutherland/> [Accessed 17 January 2017].

Fisher, Mark. 2018. *K-Punk*. Place of pub?: Repeater.

Gauthier, David. 2018. 'On Commands and Executions: Tyrants, Spectres and Vagabonds'. In *Data Browser 06: Executing Practices*. Eds. Helen Pritchard, Magdalena Tyzlik-Carver, Eric Snodgrass. London: Open Humanities Press.

Gee, Richard. 2017. 'Social Languages'. Newlearningonline.com. <https://newlearningonline.com/literacies/chapter-15/gee-on-social-languages> [Accessed 28 April 2021].

Gere, Charlie. 2006. *Art, Time and Technology*. Oxford: Berg.

Ghosh, Amitav. 2017. *The Great Derangement*. Chicago: University of Chicago Press.

Goriunova, Olga. and Alexei Shulgin. 2008. 'Glitch'. In *Software Studies: A Lexicon*. Ed. Matthew Fuller. Cambridge, MA: MIT Press.

Goriunova, Olga. 2018. 'Digital Subjects: An Introduction'. *Subjectivity*, 12(1): 1-11.

Gray, Victoria. 2012. 'NICE LAD BROKE ROSE'. *Total Art Journal*, 1(2).

Greenwood, Mark. 2012. *Lad Broke*. [Performance].

Grietzer, Peli. 2017. 'A Theory of Vibe'. *Glass Bead*, Site 1. Logic Gate: The Politics of the Artifactual Mind. <https://www.glass-bead.org/article/a-theory-of-vibe/?lang=enview> [Accessed 3 April 2020].

Hartman, Geoffrey. 1964. *Wordsworth's Poetry 1787-1814*. New Haven: Yale University Press.

Hayles, Katherine N. 2006. 'Traumas of Code'. *Critical Inquiry*, 33(1): 136-157.

Hayles, Katherine N. 2010. *How We Became Posthuman*. Chicago: University of Chicago Press.

Heidegger, Martin. 2000. *Elucidations of Hölderlin's Poetry*. Amherst, N.Y: Humanity Books.

Heidegger, Martin. 2008. *Being and Time*. New York: HarperOne.

Hejinian, Lyn. 2000. *The Language of Inquiry*. Berkeley: University of California Press.

Helmling, Steven. 2003. 'Constellation and Critique: Adorno's Constellation, Benjamin's Dialectical Image'. *Postmodern Culture*, 14(1).

Hodgson, Andrew. 2019. *The Post-War Experimental Novel*. London: Bloomsbury.

Hoffman, Michael J. 1965. 'Gertrude Stein's "Portraits."' *Twentieth Century Literature*, 11(3): 115-122.

Hot Readings. 2017. [video] Directed by Erica Scourti. https://www.youtube.com/watch?v=Kkqa99IR9IA: Sonic Acts.

House, Brian. 2017. 'Machine Listening'. *A Peer-Reviewed Journal About Machine Research*, 6(1): 16-24.

J. D. 2008. *Bullets Were Baptised.* [image] <https://www.youtube.com/watch?v=CHmUG7BLpik> [Accessed 28 April 2021].

Jackson, Virginia and Yopie Prins. Eds. 2013. *The Lyric Theory Reader.* Baltimore: Johns Hopkins University Press.

Jarvis, Simon. 2007. *Theodor W. Adorno.* London: Routledge.

Johnson, Jeff T. 2019. 'Janky materiality'. Jacket2.org. <https://jacket2.org/article/janky-materiality> [Accessed 12 April 2021].

Joyce, James. 2012. *Finnegans Wake*. Oxford: Oxford University Press.

Kember, Sarah and Joanna Zylinska. 2015. *Life After New Media*. Cambridge, MA: MIT Press.

Kenney, Martin and John Zysman. 2016. 'The Rise of the Platform Economy'. *Issues in Science and Technology*, 32(3): 61-69

Kim, Sung Wook and Aziz Douai. 2012. 'Google vs. China's "Great Firewall": Ethical Implications for Free Speech and Sovereignty'. *Technology in Society*, 34(2): 174-181.

Kittler, Freidrich. 1999. *Gramophone, Film, Typewriter.* Stanford: Stanford University Press.

Kunin, Aaron. 2017. *Jacket 40 – Late 2010* – 'Dialog on Love: Ben Lerner and Aaron Kunin in conversation'. Jacketmagazine.com. <http://jacketmagazine.com/40/lerner-kunin.shtml> [Accessed 6 November 2017].

Kunzru, Hari. 2020. *RED PILL*. New York: Simon and Schuster.

Kurke, Leslie. 2013. *The Traffic in Praise*. Berkeley, CA: Dept of Classics, University of California.

Lerner, Ben. 2010. *Mean Free Path*. New York: Copper Canyon Press.

Lerner, Ben. 2015. *10:04*. New York: Emblem.

Lim, Vivien K. G. 2002. 'The IT Way of Loafing on the Job: Cyberloafing, Neutralizing and Organizational Justice'. *Journal of Organizational Behavior*, 23(5): 675-694.

Lin, Tao. 2012. 'An Interview with Ben Lerner'. *Believer* Magazine. <https://believermag.com/an-interview-with-ben-lerner-2/> [Accessed 24 April 2021].

Link, David. 2012. *LoveLetters_1.0 MUC=Resurrection. A Memorial.* [Installation].

Lock, Frances. 2021. 'THINKING THE WORKING-CLASS 'AVEN'T GARD'. *Journal of British and Irish Innovative Poetry*, 13(1), np <online https://poetry.openlibhums.org/article/id/4372/> [Accessed 30 July 2021].

Manovich, Lev. 2000. *The Language of New Media*. Cambridge, MA: MIT Press.

Marenko, Betti. 2015. 'When Making Becomes Divination: Uncertainty and Contingency in Computational Glitch-events#. *Design Studies*, 41:110-125.

Marx, Karl and Friedrich Engels. 1848. *Manifesto of the Communist Party*. Marxists.org. <https://www.marxists.org/archive/marx/works/1848/communist-manifesto/> [Accessed 28 April 2021].

Mays, Michael. 1998. '*Finnegans Wake*, Colonial Nonsense, and Postcolonial History'. *College Literature*, 25(3), (Fall): 20-35.

McCaffery, Steve and B. P. Nichols. 1992. *Rational Geomancy*. Vancouver, B.C.: Talonbooks.

McKinty, Adrian. 2019. *The Chain*. New York: Mulholland Books.

Meakin, David. 2019. *Concussion Protocols*. Prague: Alienist.

Menkman, Rosa. 2010. *A Vernacular of File Formats*. Rosa-menkman.blogspot.co.uk. <http://rosa-menkman.blogspot.co.uk/2010/08/vernacular-of-file-formats-2-workshop.html> [Accessed 19 February 2018].

Menkman, Rosa. 2010. *Glitch Studies Manifesto*. < https://beyondresolution.info/Glitch-Studies-Manifesto> [Accessed 3 October 2021].

Menkman, Rosa. 2011. *The Glitch Moment(um)*. Amsterdam: Institute of Network Cultures.

Michaud, Jon. 2017. 'The Alternative Facts of Samuel Beckett's *Watt*'. *The New Yorker*. <https://www.newyorker.com/books/second-read/the-alternative-facts-of-samuel-becketts-watt> [Accessed 11 March 2021].

Middleton, Peter. 2015. 'Warring Clans, Podsolized Ground: Language in Contemporary UK Poetry'. In *Modernist Legacies: Trends and Faultlines in British Poetry Today*. Eds. David Nowell Smith and Abigail Lang. London: Palgrave Macmillan, 17-27.

Miyazaki, Shintaro. 2012. 'Algorhythmics: Understanding Micro-Temporality in Computational Cultures'. *Computational Culture*, 2.

Montfort, Nick. 2014. *Megawatt*. Cambridge, MA: Bad Quarto Press.

Moradi, Iman. 2009. *Glitch*. New York: Mark Batty.

Morris, Adalaide and Thomas Swiss. 2006. *New Media Poetics: Contexts, Technotexts and Theories*. Cambridge, MA: MIT Press.

Nowell Smith, David. 2013. *Sounding/Silence: Martin Heidegger at the Limit of Poetics*. New York: Fordham University Press.

Parisi, Luciana. and Stamatia Portanova. 2012. 'Soft Thought (in Architecture and Choreography)'. *Computational Culture* 1.

Parrish, Allison. 2020. *Compass Poems*. Bombmagazine.org. <https://bombmagazine.org/articles/compass-poems/> [Accessed 28 April 2021].

Peace, David. 2004. *GB84*. London: Faber and Faber.

Pierre, D. B. C. 2020. *Meanwhile in Dopamine City*. London: Faber and Faber.

Potter, Roy Claire. 2014. *Mental Furniture*. Hastings: VerySmallKitchen.

Raley, Rita. 2009. *Tactical Media*. Minneapolis: University of Minnesota Press.

Reed, Brian M. 2006. *Hart Crane: After His Lights*. Tuscaloosa, AL: University Alabama Press.

Reed, Brian M. 2011. 'In Other Words: Postmillennial Poetry and Redirected Language'. *Contemporary Literature*, 52(4): 756-790.

Riviere, Sam. 2015. *Kim Kardashian's Marriage*. London: Faber and Faber.

Rooney, Sally. 2017. *Conversations with Friends*. London: Faber and Faber.

Russell, Legacy. 2020. *Glitch Feminism: A Manifesto*. London: Verso.

Saint, Nick. 2010. 'Eric Schmidt: Google's Policy Is to "Get Right Up To The Creepy Line And Not Cross It"'. *Business Insider.* <https://www.businessinsider.com/eric-schmidt-googles-policy-is-to-get-right-up-to-the-creepy-line-and-not-cross-it-2010-10?r=US&IR=T> [Accessed 23 April 2021].

Salisbury, Laura. 2014. 'Gloria SMH and Beckett's Linguistic Encryptions'. In *Edinburgh Companion to Samuel Beckett and The Arts*, 1st ed. Ed. Stanley E. Gontarski. Edinburgh: Edinburgh University Press, 153-169.

Satrom, Jon. 2012. *Prepared Desktop: Plugin BeachBall Success Jon Satrom TM2K12.* [video] <https://www.youtube.com/watch?v=6jrz45AK-yA> [Accessed 25 April 2021].

Schaffer, Janek. 1995. *Recorded Delivery.* [Installation].

Schwartz, Alexandra. 2017. 'A New Kind of Adultery Novel'. *The New Yorker.* <https://www.newyorker.com/magazine/2017/07/31/a-new-kind-of-adultery-novel> [Accessed 28 April 2021].

Scourti, Erica. 2015. *Erica Scourti.* [online] Ericascourti.com. <http://www.ericascourti.com/> [Accessed 24 April 2021].

Simmers, Claire. and Murugan Anandarajan. 2018. *The Internet of People, Things and Services.* New York: Routledge.

Spritz. 2016. *Spritz.* <https://spritz.com> [Accessed 24 April 2021].

Stein, Gertrude. 1922. *Geography and Plays*. Boston: Four Seas Co.

Stein, Gertrude. 1978. *How to Write*. New York: Dover Publications.

Stewart, Garrett. 2015. 'Tongue #2'. In *Torque #2: The Act of Reading*. Eds. Nathan and Sam Skinner. Liverpool: Torque.

Sutherland, Keston. 2010. 'Wrong Poetry'. *Textual Practice*, 24(4): 765-782.

Sutherland, Keston. 2013. *The Odes to TL61P.* London: Enitharmon Press.

Sutherland, Ross G. 2011. *EVERY RENDITION ON A BROKEN MACHINE.* [online] Every-rendition. tumblr.com. <https://every-rendition.tumblr.com> [Accessed 24 April 2021].

Stupart, Linda. 2016. *Virus.* London: Arcadia Missa.

Tamplin, John. 2015. 'Keston Sutherland interview with John Tamplin'. Manifold.group.shef.ac.uk. <http://www.manifold.group.shef.ac.uk/issue17/KestonSutherlandJohnTamplinBM17.html> [Accessed 24 May 2018].

Temkin, Daniel and Hugh S. Manon. 2011. 'Notes on Glitch'. Worldpicturejournal.com. <http://www.worldpicturejournal.com/WP_6/Manon.html> [Accessed 25 June 2018].

Temkin, Daniel. 2021. 'What Programming Language Would Yoko Ono Create?' esoteric.codes. <https://esoteric.codes/blog/what-programming-language-would-yoko-ono-write> [Accessed 23 April 2021].

Temkin, Daniel. n.d. [online] esoteric.codes. <https://esoteric.codes> [Accessed 23 April 2021].

Tenenbaum, Louis. 1986. 'From Futurism to Pacifism: Aldo Palazzeschi and the First World War'. *Italica*, 63(4):386-394

Thomas, Abigail. 2012. 'Bob Brown's Reading Machine & the Imagined Escape from the Page'. P-dpa.net. <http://p-dpa.net/bob-browns-reading-machine/> [Accessed 24 April 2021].

Thomas, Jennett. 2013. *The Unspeakable Freedom Device.* [video] <https://jennetthomas.wordpress.com/videos/the-unspeakable-freedom-device/> [Accessed 28 April 2021].

Thomas, J. 2015. *The Unspeakable Freedom Device.* London: Book Works.

Thornton, Pip. 2019. *Language in the Age of Algorithmic Reproduction: A Critique of Linguistic Capitalism*. PhD. Royal Holloway University of London.

Thurston, Scott. 2011. *Talking Poetics*. Exeter: Shearsman Books.

Trecartin, Ryan. 2013. *Centre Jenny*. [video] <https://vimeo.com/75735816> [Accessed 28 April 2021].

Virno, Paulo. 2001. *A Grammar of the Multitude*. Los Angeles: Semiotext(e).

Waldrup-Fruin, Noah. 2011. 'Digital Media Archaeology: Interpreting Computational Processes'. In *Media Archaeology: Approaches, Applications, and Implications*. Eds. Erkki Huhtamo and Jussi Parikka. Berkeley: University of California Press, 302-322.

Weiß, M. 2015. 'What is Computer Art? An attempt towards an answer and examples of interpretation'. [online] Medienkunstnetz.de. <http://www.medienkunstnetz.de/themes/generative-tools/computer_art/14/#ftn60> [Accessed 28 April 2021].

Williams, Raymond. 1977. *Marxism and Literature*. Oxford: Oxford University Press.

Williams, Raymond. 2010. *Culture and Materialism: Selected Essays* (New ed.). London: Verso.

Zalasiewicz, Jan, Colin Waters, Colin Summerhayes and Mark Williams. 2018. 'The Anthropocene'. *Geology Today*, 34(5): 177-181.

Zimmer, Ben. 2013. 'The Hidden History of 'Glitch' : Word Routes : Thinkmap Visual Thesaurus'. [online] Visualthesaurus.com. <https://www.visualthesaurus.com/cm/wordroutes/the-hidden-history-of-glitch> [Accessed 19 February 2018].

www.ingramcontent.com/pod-product-compliance
Lightning Source LLC
LaVergne TN
LVHW091116080826
845145LV00008B/1945
* 9 7 8 1 7 8 5 4 2 1 1 4 3 *